The IEA Health and Welfare Unit

Choice in Welfare No. 24

Just a Piece of Paper?
Divorce Reform and the
Undermining of Marriage

James Q. Wilson
Melanie Phillips
Patricia Morgan
Norman Barry
Bryce Christensen

Robert Whelan (Editor)

IEA Health and Welfare Unit
London, 1995

First published July 1995

The IEA Health and Welfare Unit
2 Lord North St
London SW1P 3LB

ISBN 0-255 36361-3

Front cover clipart from
Totem Graphics Inc and CorelDRAW 5

Typeset by the IEA Health and Welfare Unit
in New Century Schoolbook 10 on 11 point
Printed in Great Britain by
St Edmundsbury Press Ltd
Blenheim Industrial Park, Newmarket Rd
Bury St Edmunds, Suffolk

Contents

Foreword

For years opponents of marriage have dismissed it as 'just a piece of paper'. Despite this hostility, the majority of families have continued to regard marriage as a lifelong commitment, and not a mere agreement for the time being. The Government's misguided divorce reforms, however, will succeed in finally reducing marriage to little more than the proverbial 'scrap of paper'.

The Lord Chancellor's White Paper, *Looking to the Future: Mediation and the Ground for Divorce*, contains statements of firm support for marriage which are intended to be reassuring, but each legal landmark on the road to the enfeebling of marriage—not least the 1969 Divorce Reform Act—has been accompanied by similar assurances of support for holy matrimony. None of these assurances has meant anything in practice and neither will those of the Lord Chancellor. The proposed law is about tidying up the mess left by separating couples. But law at its best has a tutelary role. It is an affirmation of what is just and right in human affairs, in the hope of bringing out the best in people. And for good reason.

As the champions of liberty from Adam Smith onwards have long understood, a society of free and responsible individuals rests on individual virtues. And the virtues indispensable to liberty are acquired primarily in the family. To weaken the family is therefore of no small importance.

No successful society known to human experience has ever taken lightly the obligations of parents towards their own children. The cost of their financial upkeep is the least of the matter. What is truly important is that the biological parents are committed to giving up their own time and energy to developing the character of their own offspring. Compared with this responsibility, whether the couple like each other more or less than any alternative partner, is of trivial importance.

Divorce law should be the means by which a society signals its support for the special importance of adults devoting themselves to the upkeep and nurture of their own children. The Government's proposals, however, diminish the special quality of the bond between parents and their children, reducing it to the status of a side-effect of parental likes and dislikes.

A Government which cannot see what is at stake, truly lacks what George Bush revealingly called the 'vision thing'.

Dr David G. Green

The Authors

Norman Barry has been Professor of Politics at the University of Buckingham since 1984. Previously he was Senior Lecturer in Government at the City of Birmingham Polytechnic (now the University of Central England). He specialises in social and political theory and his books include *Hayek's Social and Economic Philosophy*, 1979; *Welfare*, 1990 and *The Morality of Business Enterprise,* 1991 and *An Introduction to Modern Political Theory*, third edition 1995. He has contributed to many periodicals and learned journals. He was Visiting Scholar at the Social Philosophy and Policy Centre, Bowling Green State University, Ohio.

Professor Barry is a member of the Academic Advisory Councils of the Institute of Economic Affairs and the David Hume Institute (Edinburgh).

Bryce Christensen is editor of *The Family in America* and associate director of The Rockford Institute Center on the Family in America, a research organisation devoted to the investigation of cultural, economic, ethical and political issues affecting family life in the USA. He is the author of *Utopia Against the Family*, 1990; (editor) *The Family Wage*, 1988; *Day Care: Child Psychology and Adult Economics*, 1989; *The Retreat from Marriage*, 1990 and *When Families Fail...The Social Costs*, 1991.

Dr Christensen has been widely published by newspapers and scholarly journals in the USA, focusing on the family, parental rights and demographic trends.

Patricia Morgan, Senior Research Fellow on the family at the IEA's Health and Welfare Unit, is a sociologist specialising in criminology and family policy. She is the author or co-author of a number of books including: *Delinquent Phantasies*, 1978; *Facing Up to Family Income*, 1989; *The Hidden Costs of Childcare*, 1992; *Families in Dreamland*, 1992. Her book *Farewell to the Family?*, published by the IEA Health and Welfare Unit in January 1995, achieved national media coverage. She has contributed chapters to *Full Circle, Family Portraits,* and *The Loss of Virtue*, as well as articles for periodicals and national newspapers.

Patricia Morgan is a frequent contributor to television and radio programmes and is presently writing a full-length work on the relationship between capitalism and the family.

Melanie Phillips is a columnist for *The Observer*, where she writes about social affairs and political culture. She moved to *The Observer* in 1993 after working for 16 years for *The Guardian*. She is author of *Divided House*, a study of women at Westminster, and co-author with Dr John Dawson of *Doctors' Dilemmas*, a primer on medical ethics.

Robert Whelan is the Assistant Director of the IEA's Health and Welfare Unit. He has written and produced a series of videos on social and medical issues including *The Truth about Aids, Facing Facts on Population* and *The Three R's of Family Life*. He has written and spoken widely on issues relating to population and the environment, and his essay *Mounting Greenery* was published by the IEA's Education Unit.

James Q. Wilson, since 1985 the Collins Professor of Management and Public Policy at UCLA was for twenty-six years the Shattuck Professor of Government at Harvard University. Among his books are *The Moral Sense,* 1994 and *On Character,* 1995.

Editor's Introduction

Robert Whelan

WHEN London Zoo was threatened with closure, the columnist Auberon Waugh added his voice to those who were campaigning on its behalf. He argued that the preservation of the zoo was essential as it gave wild animals the opportunity to study the behaviour of divorced men who take their children there on Sunday afternoons. How else, he asked, are we to impress upon the brute creation the importance of fidelity and monogamy?

How indeed? But some of those animals have spent long lifetimes in the zoo, and must have noticed a sharp increase over the years in the number of divorced fathers who visit them. Within living memory, divorce has changed from being something unusual to being a common occurrence of modern life.

In 1992 there were 160,000 divorces, representing a divorce rate of 13.7 per one thousand married people. This marked a new peak in the statistics, but that in itself was not surprising. Divorce has been increasing rapidly for so long now that the same could be said of every year's figures. In 1960 there were just under 24,000 divorces and a rate of 2.0 per one thousand married people—and 1960 is not exactly another country, separated from us by the passage of generations.

The government helpfully publishes statistics on marriage and divorce in the same volume, thus enabling us to see that the obverse of record highs in divorce is a record low in marriage. In 1992 there were 311,000 marriages, down from 343,000 in 1960 and 415,000 in 1970. Owing to an increase in the population of marriageable males and females over the period, the drop in terms of rates has been even steeper. In 1960, for every one thousand men over 16, 77 got married for the first time. By 1970 it was 86. In 1992 it was 37. For women the figures were 82, 100 and 47 respectively. Marriage rates are at their lowest level since the state began to collect statistics on marriage over a century and a half ago.

In fact, the fall in the popularity of marriage has been so spectacular that there are *fewer first marriages now in absolute numbers* than there were a hundred years ago. In 1992, out of 311,000 marriages in England and Wales, 191,000 were first marriages, but in 1892 out of 227,000 marriages there were 192,000 first marriages.[1] This is truly extraordinary when we consider that the population has increased by three quarters over the period.

Giving Up On Marriage

So how can we account for the widespread abandonment of the institution which has provided the foundations for the social order in every known human society? Dr Johnson once observed that 'every man is a worse man in proportion as he is unfit for the married state', and he believed that, in spite of the obvious risks and drawbacks, 'Marriage has many pains, but celibacy no pleasure'. The Johnsonian aphorism has less relevance now, as the alternative to marriage is not celibacy but cohabitation. The extent to which cohabitation is practised, and the possibility that it might either challenge or replace marriage as the social norm, is currently occupying demographers and social scientists.[2] By definition, cohabitation is informal, lacking the state-registered ceremonies which mark the beginning and end of marriage, but there is little doubt of its increasing popularity. In 1991-2 30 per cent of single women aged 25-34 were cohabiting.[3]

The decline of marriage and the rise of divorce are directly linked because, as Patricia Morgan points out in this volume, the liberalising of divorce legislation alters the nature of the contract it terminates. As divorce becomes more easily available so more people will resort to it as an escape from difficult situations: divorce becomes the first option rather than the last. With divorce available effectively on demand and without the consent of the other partner, the incentive to invest resources—both personal and financial—in a relationship is diminished. Marriage becomes temporary and provisional rather than binding and permanent. It may be used by one or both parties as a base from which to make forays into pools of possible alternative partners, searching for something younger/richer/sexier or just nicer.

Under the circumstances, it is hardly surprising that increasing numbers of men and women choose not to marry at all. One long-standing criticism of marriage as a legal entity used to be that it was 'just a piece of paper', a formal document which could never express the essentially romantic nature of the relationship. But now marriage does not even function like other legal pieces of paper, because it has become a contract which is unenforced and unenforceable. As Norman Barry points out in this book, in all other areas of contract law those who break a contract are expected to compensate their partner or partners for their disappointed expectations, but under a system of 'no fault' divorce, this essential element of contract law is abrogated. Divorce comes to be regarded as one of those things that just happens—it's nobody's guilt.

Those who oppose the liberalising of divorce are sometimes accused of wanting to trap unhappy people in violent, abusive or exploitive relationships. However, the alternative to liberal or 'no fault' divorce is not no divorce, but divorce which is granted only for the most serious reasons and after due legal process to establish fault.

The Elimination of Fault

Prior to the Reformation the church upheld marriage as a lifelong commitment, with the result that divorce was simply impossible to obtain (although the Church did—and still does—allow annulments where the marriage could be shown to be sacramentally invalid.) In the more secular society which followed the Reformation divorce became available, but only for the rich and powerful, as a private Act of Parliament was required.

The 1857 Matrimonial Causes Act allowed divorce on the basis of clearly defined evidence of immoral behaviour such as adultery, bigamy, sodomy, cruelty or desertion. The 1937 Matrimonial Causes Act enlarged the grounds for divorce, but still maintained the critical demand for proof of guilt. The major change came with the 1969 Divorce Reform Act which ushered in divorce on the sole ground that the marriage had broken down 'irretrievably'. This could be demonstrated by one of five 'facts': adultery, unreasonable behaviour, desertion, two years separation with consent or five years separation without consent. While it is true that the first three 'facts' were still fault-based, in the sense that they related to the behaviour of the partners, the critical bridge had been crossed. The 'facts' are not the grounds for divorce: they only provide evidence of 'irretrievable' breakdown, and as the Lord Chancellor's White Paper admits:

...the evidence required is not of the same weight as that which was required before the law was reformed in 1969. Under the old law, a high degree of proof was required and a petition for divorce would fail if the petitioner had connived at the commission of the offence or colluded with the respondent in any way. The position today is quite different.[4]

If the breakdown of the marriage was 'irretrievable', then there was no part for the law to play in trying to shore it up by making divorce difficult to obtain or by refusing it. Furthermore, the decision as to whether or not the marriage had reached such a stage was to be left, in some cases at least, to the subjective judgement of the parties, with no external standards applied.

In 1973 a Special Procedure was introduced to allow couples to divorce without even appearing in court. It is now used for 99 per cent of undefended divorces. As George Brown has said, divorce is now almost as simple to obtain as a TV licence:[5]

Qualitatively, divorce has changed from being a distinctly moral matter with a guilty party, an offended party and consequent stigma, to an administrative arrangement judged by administrative criteria of the speed and cheapness of court proceedings with little interest shown in whether the marriage has indeed irretrievably broken down, next to no concern for a wronged 'divorced' party and little effort at reconciliation.[6]

An interesting contribution to the debate surrounding divorce in recent years has come from Ruth Deech, a barrister and now Principal of St Anne's College, Oxford. Her first post, after being called to the Bar in 1967, was with the Law Commission which was formulating what was to become the Divorce Reform Act 1969. She is therefore able to write, from personal experience, of the processes which led up to the passage of this most momentous piece of anti-marriage legislation. In her pamphlet for the Centre for Policy Studies, *Divorce Dissent,* she claims that:

It is now clear that the work of the reformers in the 1960s was flawed. Their reliance on selected statistics and works of social science led to wholly inaccurate predictions about the effect of the Divorce Reform Act 1969.[7]

In every respect, the supposed benefits of divorce law liberalisation failed to materialise. The stated aims of the Act, with its principle of 'no fault' divorce, were to promote 'the stability of marriage, reconciliation, maximum fairness, protection of children and the economically weaker spouse', together with a reduction in the out-of-wedlock birth rate, as it was claimed that many parents would have married prior to the birth of their children if only they had not been trapped in previous marriages by unbending divorce legislation.[8] However:

The most pronounced failure of the reform of the 1960s was the prediction of the level of the divorce rate itself. It was thought that there would not be a large increase and that the rates might even fall back. In fact the rate trebled from approximately 60,000 petitions a year in the late 1960s to 190,000 per annum today.[9]

Ignoring the Lessons of History

The reason for recalling these failed predictions of the 1960s is that the same arguments are advanced every time further liberalisation of the divorce law is mooted, and we are currently hearing them re-run yet again in support of the Lord Chancellor Lord Mackay's White Paper *Looking to the Future*.[10] In particular, the peculiar notion that liberalising divorce law does not lead to more divorces, but only to the decent burial of some already dead marriages before any more harm is done, has proved to be perennially popular with the reformers. But as Ruth Deech points out:

... every reform of the law in the last 130 years, whatever the reason, has led to an irreversible rise in the divorce rate ... The divorce rate went up in the late 1940s when legal aid was extended to divorce; it went up dramatically after the passage of the 1969 Divorce Reform Act and has continued to climb, especially after the reform of procedure in 1977. Over and again in this century reformers have told us that the law has to be amended to bring it into line with reality ... The black letter law is then brought into line with practice; the divorce rate rises and very soon we find that practice is again out of step with the law. Somewhere a stop has to be called.[11]

Before the Lord Chancellor's White Paper there was a Green Paper, published in December 1993, and that in turn grew out of demands for divorce law reform from the Law Commission, which published a discussion paper in May 1988 and a final report and recommendations in November 1990.[12] The Commission made the claim that:

> ...the number of divorces does not, as is sometimes alleged, indicate any fundamental weakening of the fabric of society.[13]

This seems a bizarre stance to adopt, given the volume of research which links divorce with poor outcomes for both adults and children, and the scale on which divorce is now occurring. There is now one divorce for every two marriages, and Britain has the highest divorce rate in the European Union. Over a quarter of all households are single person households, and the fastest growing group within this sector are men under retirement age—the very people who would, until recently, have been expected to form part of a family.[14] With so many isolated men, either divorced or never married, and consequently not bound into the social fabric by the ties of family responsibilities, some commentators have predicted the emergence of a 'warrior class'.[15]

At the time of the Law Commission's proposals, the Law Commissioner with responsibility for family law was Professor Brenda Hoggett QC (now Mrs Justice Hale). In 1980, whilst a member of the Faculty of Law at Manchester University, she had written:

> Family law no longer makes any attempt to buttress the stability of marriage or any other union. It has adopted principles for the protection of children and dependent spouses which could be made equally applicable to the unmarried. In such circumstances, the piecemeal erosion of the distinction between marriage and non-marital cohabitation may be expected to continue. Logically, we have already reached a point at which, rather than discussing which remedies should now be extended to the unmarried, we should be considering whether the legal institution of marriage continues to serve any useful purposes.[16]

Nobody's Fault

The Lord Chancellor's proposals for divorce law reform, which were based on the recommendations of the Law Commission of which Mrs Hoggett was a member, would seem to give a definite 'No' to her question. The issue of fault, already very weak in divorce proceedings, will be removed altogether.

... the Government proposes that the ground for divorce should be the irretrievable breakdown of the marriage as demonstrated by the sole fact of a period of reflection and consideration.[17]

This period of reflection and consideration will last for twelve months from the filing of the petition. In the absence of any other evidence that the marriage has indeed broken down irretrievably this twelve month gap acquires great significance, and indeed the Lord Chancellor appears to have invested the exact length of it with an almost magical symbolism. A shorter period would mean that 'a divorce could be granted without any adequate reflection and consideration', while a longer period 'would act as an encouragement to walk out of the marriage ... before fulfilling the obligations and responsibilities towards the previous marriage and children'.[18] But twelve months is, like Baby Bear's porridge, just right. It is difficult to see any compelling reason for such an assumption.

Under the White Paper's proposals the behaviour of the parties will no longer have any relevance, as the 'proof' of irretrievable breakdown will depend upon nothing more than the subjective view of whoever is making the claim:

If spouses are prepared to swear to the belief that the marriage has broken down...and then, a considerable time later, they reiterate the view that the breakdown in their relationship is irreparable, there can scarcely be any better proof that the marriage is at an end.[19]

The White Paper complains of 'the damage done by the present encouragement to rely on facts that require allegations of fault',[20] which seems a bizarre position to receive support from the country's chief law officer. No doubt there are many defendants appearing in the dock every day who would be glad to escape 'the damage done by ... facts that require allegations of fault', but we take it to be the role of the courts to establish guilt and innocence.

The White Paper justifies its dropping of fault as a basis for divorce by pointing out that, at the moment, about 75 per cent of divorce petitions cite adultery or unreasonable behaviour, whilst fewer than 20 per cent of divorces go through on the rule of two years separation with consent of both parties, and fewer than 6 per cent on the five years separation without consent.[21] The interpretation of this is that people cite fault in order to get quicker divorces, the median time between divorce petition and decree absolute at the moment being about six months.[22] No consideration seems to have been given to the possibility that people getting divorced make allegations of fault out of a sense of injury and a desire for justice. As George Brown has pointed out, '... the lawyers' no-fault divorce is at odds with people's common understanding that fault is involved'.[23]

Sailing in Uncharted Waters

In 1956 the last Royal Commission to deal with the subject reported that:

> ... to give people a right to divorce themselves would be to foster a change in the attitude to marriage which would be disastrous for the nation...marriage in the end would come to be regarded as a temporary relationship with divorce as a normal incident of life...people have good and bad impulses and we conceive it to be the function of the law to strengthen the good and control the bad.

There is a certain irony in the fact that Lord Mackay, with his strict Presbyterian background and his personal commitment to the view that marriage should be for life,[24] could be the Lord Chancellor to turn the Royal Commission's nightmare vision into a reality. Should his White Paper be enacted into law, we would indeed have a situation in which people can divorce themselves and in which marriage would be regarded as no more than a temporary relationship.

The long-term consequences are difficult to predict. As Patricia Morgan has argued in *Farewell to the Family?*, there is no society known to anthropology which has not been based on marriage:

> All societies that have survived have been built on marriage, and children have always been raised within 'traditional' families. Even if some societies have had polygamy, and a few polyandry, while in others a number of married couples have lived in one household, it still remains a truism that: 'Not only has there never been an open, democratic society not based on the family, there has never been any society of any sort not based on the family'.[25]

Having dissolved marriage as the basis of the social order, we are now sailing in uncharted waters. The links between the collapse of the traditional family based on marriage and social pathologies such as crime, low educational achievement, mental and physical ill health and reduced economic activity are now well known. The marked decline in the quality of life which we have experienced in the last quarter century is now only too apparent, and the classic permissive response that 'the family isn't declining, only changing' is heard less often. However, we have no means of knowing where the trends will bottom out, in the absence of any historical model of a society in which, to use Brenda Hoggett's phrase, the 'law no longer makes any attempt to buttress the stability of marriage'.

Many people have attempted to put a figure on the cost of marital breakdown to the country. The estimates have varied from millions to billions, because it all depends on what you include in the calculation. Costs such as legal aid for divorce and payments to families headed by lone parents are fairly easy to obtain, but other costs are more difficult to quantify. If the traditional family, headed by married parents who commit themselves to each other for life, is the principal cultural conduit through which values are transmitted to the next generation, then the destruction of such a mechanism implies costs which are truly incalculable. It is perhaps no accident that the educational authorities have been placing such emphasis on education for citizenship in recent years, because the home, which has traditionally been the nursery of good citizens, is no longer up to the task for many children. Whether this deficit can be made good through agencies of the state is a profoundly worrying question.

In this collection of essays the authors examine a number of aspects of divorce law and its consequences. Melanie Phillips concentrates of the abolition of fault, and the 'no pain, no blame, no shame' concept of justice which lies at the heart of the White Paper. Patricia Morgan examines the evidence on the relationship between conflict and divorce, and comes to the conclusion that not only does divorce not bring conflict to an end, it may mark the beginning of an even more bitter phase, especially for children. Norman Barry's chapter on 'Justice and Liberty in Marriage and Divorce' first appeared in our book *Liberating Women...From Modern Feminism*.[26] It is reprinted here as his account of the way in which marriage has been deprived of its meaning both as a vow and as a contract is highly relevant to the proposals of the White Paper. Finally we are pleased to include two contributions from authors in the USA, where permissive divorce legislation has antedated trends in this country by several years. Bryce Christensen's review of the consequences of twenty years of no fault divorce first appeared in *The Family in America*, the journal of the Rockford Institute. James Q. Wilson's essay 'The Family-Values Debate', which first appeared in *Commentary* in 1993, has come to be regarded as a classic exposition of what he describes as 'the war over what the family is'. His view that the essence of marriage is commitment, and that 'married life is shaped by the fact that the couple has made a solemn vow ... that this is for keeps' is also highly relevant to current proposals for divorce law reform in Britain.

The Lord Chancellor and Marriage

When discussing the issue of arranged marriages, Samuel Johnson once said:

> I believe marriages would in general be as happy, and often more so, if they were all made by the Lord Chancellor, upon a due consideration of the characters and circumstances, without the parties having any choice in the matter.

Whatever one's views on arranged marriages, it is doubtful if many people would wish to leave such a choice to the Lord Chancellor today. However, marriages may be marred as well as made by the law officers, and Lord Mackay's White Paper, if enacted into law, would represent that last step in a long process which has seen the laws relating to marriage and its dissolution drained of any moral content. It would be unreasonably optimistic to assume that such a process can be carried through without entailing the most severe social consequences.

Notes

1   All long-term historical statistics are taken from OPCS, *Marriage and Divorce Statistics: Historical series of statistics on marriage and divorce in England and Wales, 1837-1983*, Series FM2, No. 16, London: HMSO, 1990. More recent statistics are taken from OPCS, *Marriage and Divorce Statistics 1992: England and Wales*, Series FM2, No. 20, London: HMSO, 1994.

2   see Dormor, D.J., *The Relationship Revolution: Cohabitation, Marriage and Divorce in Contemporary Europe*, London: One Plus One; Kiernan, K.E. and Estaugh, V., *Cohabitation: Extra-Marital Childbearing and Social Policy*, London: Family Policy Studies Centre, 1993.

3   Central Statistical Office, *Social Trends 25*, London: HMSO, 1995, p. 39.

4   Lord Chancellor's Department, *Looking to the Future: Mediation and the Ground for Divorce*, Cm 2799, London: HMSO, 1995, para. 2.10.

5   Brown, G., *The Decay of Marriage*, Milton Keynes: Family Education Trust, 1991, p. 23.

6   Brown, G., *Finding Fault in Divorce*, London: Social Affairs Unit, 1989, p. 3.

7   Deech, R., *Divorce Dissent: Dangers in Divorce Reform*, London: Centre for Policy Studies, 1994, p. 10.

8   *Ibid.*

9   *Ibid.*, p. 11.

10 Lord Chancellor's Department, *Looking to the Future: Mediation and the Ground For Divorce*, Cm 2799, London: HMSO, 1995.

11 Deech, R., *op. cit.*, pp. 8 and 12.

12 *Facing the Future*, Law Commission No. 170, London, 1988; *The Ground for Divorce*, Law Commission No. 192, London, 1990.

13 *Facing the Future, op. cit.*, para 2.22.

14 'The growth in the proportion of one person households has been among people under pensionable age living alone, particularly men. By 2001, nearly one in ten households in Great Britain are projected to comprise a man under pensionable age living alone compared with only one in thirty in 1971'. OPCS, *Social Trends 25*, London: HMSO, 1995, p. 30. See also Haskey, J., 'Trends in Marriage, Cohabitation and Living Outside a Partnership', *Population Trends 80*, London: HMSO, 1995.

15 see Morgan, P., *Farewell to the Family? Public Policy and Family Breakdown in Britain and the USA*, London: IEA Health and Welfare Unit, 1995, pp. 143-46.

16 Hoggett, B., 'Ends and Means: The Utility of Marriage as a Legal Institution', in Eekelaar, J.M., and Catz, S. (eds.), *Marriage and Cohabitation in Contemporary Societies*, Butterworth, 1980, p. 101.

17 *Looking to the Future*, 1995, *op. cit.*, para 4.7.

18 *Ibid.*, para 4.13.

19 *Ibid.*, para 2.36.

20 *Ibid.*, para 4.34.

21 *Ibid.*, para 2.4.

22 *Ibid.*, para 4.15.

23 Brown, G., *Finding Fault in Divorce*, *op. cit.*, p. 19.

24 *Looking to the Future*, 1995, *op. cit.*, p. iii.

25 Morgan, P., *Farewell to the Family: Public Policy and Family Breakdown in Britain and the USA*, London: IEA Health and Welfare Unit, 1995, p. 152, quoting Levy, M., *Feminism and Freedom*, Transaction, 1987, p. 284.

26 Quest, C. (ed.), *Liberating Women...From Modern Feminism*, London: IEA Health and Welfare Unit, 1994.

Death Blow to Marriage

Melanie Phillips

By common consent the Lord Chancellor Lord Mackay, is regarded as a man of the most stern and unbending uprightness. A moral relativist he is not. Indeed, as an adherent of an arcane Scottish Presbyterian sect, he subscribes to strict and rigidly enforced rules of behaviour. Yet he has managed to produce a White Paper on divorce that is disingenuous to the point of deceit. The spin put on it by his department is that it will help shore up marriage. In fact, the very opposite is likely to be the case. The Lord Chancellor is held in high esteem as a man of not only moral but intellectual rigour. Yet his White Paper is riddled with internal contradictions and *non sequiturs* and is even in places factually wrong.

So what has caused this strange dislocation? It appears that Lord Mackay, confronted by the several irreconcilable forces of the family law establishment's crusade to abolish marriage, the government's (ahem) crusade to uphold family values and his personal crusade to slash his department's expenditure, has been sucked into the intellectual black hole of his own perception that law is merely the helpless instrument, rather than a significant shaper, of public attitudes. On the face of it, the White Paper is a cunning political package. Does it make divorce harder or easier? It's difficult to say. Removing the concept of fault by abolishing the grounds of adultery, desertion or unreasonable behaviour appears to make it easier. On the other hand, ending 'quickie' divorces which take between three and six months and making everyone wait instead for at least a year appears to make it harder. But peering at this carefully presented paradox is merely to look at these proposals down the wrong end of the telescope. It's not what they will do to divorce that should worry us. It's what they will do to marriage.

This chapter is based on a column which appeared in *The Observer*, 8 May 1995.

The Abolition of Marriage

The abolition of fault will virtually kill marriage off as a concept with any legal meaning. Fault describes what happens when someone is held responsible for their bad behaviour. Abolishing fault abolishes the concept of personal responsibility. It effectively declares that the breakdown of the marriage is no-one's responsibility. Marital breakdown becomes instead something that just happens to unfortunate individuals, like meningitis or an earthquake. Moreover, eradicating failure to meet marital obligations eradicates the obligations themselves. Civil marriage does not set out the obligations of one spouse to another. They are inferred instead from the legal remedies in divorce. Duties such as staying together, being faithful to each other or treating each other reasonably exist only by virtue of the fault that accrues to desertion, adultery or unreasonable behaviour. Remove these defaults, and marriage becomes a vapid concept.

Aha, says the Lord Chancellor, but fault obviously doesn't exert much force at present because it is used as the trigger for the fastest kind of divorce. That's true as far as it goes, which is not very far. Fault is already an etiolated and pretty meaningless concept in divorce proceedings. That's because the current divorce law embodies the historic fudge enacted in 1969, which spatchcocked together judgementalism and non-judgementalism in the same legal package. Thus the value-neutral concept of irretrievable breakdown which became the new grounds for divorce is defined by one of five criteria, three of which—adultery, unreasonable behaviour or desertion—imply fault. In 1973 the Special Procedure was introduced which eliminates court hearings and means the divorce can be transacted at speed and entirely on paper. The result is that if someone goes along to her solicitor and says she wants a divorce, then unless the couple have been separated for two or five years the solicitor will most likely riffle through the three fault-based criteria and select the one that most closely applies. So of course fault is pretty meaningless in individual cases.

Getting rid of it altogether still matters, however, on account of the rhetorical and declaratory general effect of law upon public policy and attitudes. And fault has been eroded by more than statute. Through the development of case law since 1969, which has progressively uncoupled conduct from ancillary divorce matters, fault is not longer relevant to considerations such as the settlement of property or the custody of the children. Why not? If—as they should be—the interests of the children are paramount, why shouldn't the behaviour of the parents be one of the factors taken into consideration when custody is awarded? Dominating the White Paper, however, is the horror of apportioning blame. The system's current imposition of fault, runs its argument, raises the temperature of divorcing couples to boiling point and thus does harm. But since virtually all 'fault' divorces are transacted on paper, far from the Lord Chancellor's premise that fault causes untold misery, confrontation and hostility it does nothing of the kind. What's more, the perverse linkage with quickies could easily be abolished by abolishing quickie divorce but hanging onto the concept of fault. No, says the White Paper; this would merely prolong the misery, hostility and so on.

No Pain, No Blame Justice

This is the philosophical heart of the White Paper: the no pain, no blame, no shame justice system. There are many fallacies in this position. The prime consideration of the justice system is not the avoidance of pain. In every other area of law, it aims to make people who have done wrong accept the consequences of their actions. Denying a wronged party the opportunity to say their spouse behaved badly is inimical to justice. It tries to sanitise proceedings by getting the parties to collude in an evasion of truth and is likely to cause much more frustration and bitterness by imposing such unreality. It holds that the truth is too dangerous as it might upset people. Imagine saying of a burglar that he shouldn't be blamed for his crime because it might stigmatise him and make him upset! Imagine saying of a neighbour who tears down next door's fence that he shouldn't be held responsible and made to pay for the destruction because it would make it more difficult for the two of them to live next door to each other afterwards!

The argument runs that marital rows are all too complex and sensitive, that the law has no place trying to arbitrate in personal behaviour. But this is an argument for abolishing the whole of matrimonial law, or all anti-discrimination legislation. It runs against the whole thrust of property law where courts provide remedies over and over again for people who are victims of broken promises or betrayals of trust or agreements. The difficulty of proving a legal wrong is hardly a reason for abolishing it altogether. Yet this absurd doctrine is held to apply—solely—to divorce.

The implication is that the pain of marital breakdown somehow starts with the legal process. But the legal fight is the *result* of marital bitterness, not the cause. The idea that preventing a wronged spouse from alleging adultery will turn bitter anger into calm reason is sheer fantasy. Lord Mackay appears to believe that mediation will shore up marriage by forcing people to reflect on grim reality. Again this is deeply misleading. Mediation is not counselling or reconciliation. It is solely concerned with sorting out practicalities once the couple have made their decision to part. It assumes the divorcing couple are calm and reasonable enough to sit down with the mediator. But many are so bitter that by definition they won't even get to the mediator in the first place. And if they are reasonable, they won't need a mediator anyway. This is also likely to become a two tier system. The more powerful and rich spouse (usually the man) will get a lawyer; the weaker and poorer (the woman) will have to make do with a mediator and thus lose the legal protection that is necessary. The only pain likely to be reduced by this will be at the Treasury, where there will be rejoicing at the reduction of the legal aid bill.

Conflict and Divorce

Of course it's true that the more conflict there is, the worse it is for the children. But the White Paper seeks to wrap itself in virtue by linking abolition of fault to abolition of conflict for children. It repeats the misapprehension that it's not divorce that's harmful to children but conflict, with the implication that such conflict ends with divorce. This is utterly wrong, although much peddled as a principal alibi for the adult betrayal of children's interests. Of course conflict is harmful but the evidence shows that parental separation outweighs conflict in doing damage to children. It's separation and divorce that do most harm: harm greater than if a parent were to die. As the Cambridge child development expert Martin Richards has said, it is the parent's decision to leave a child that destroys that child's self esteem and causes relative disadvantage in virtually every area of its development.[1] There's nothing new in that finding, although it has been strenuously denied by liberal opinion until very recently. Last year's study by the Exeter child health researchers John Tripp and Monica Cockett demonstrated it unequivocally.[2] But in any event, a moment's disinterested thought would tell one that the divorce-ends-conflict theory is nonsense. Marital conflict may not only increase at divorce but often continues afterwards; worse still, such conflict may from that point centre for the first time on the children themselves. The children become the battleground on which the parents choose to fight their war.

So divorce often makes marital conflict worse for children, not better. Set against this inconvenient fact, the idea that conflict will be minimised if the law denies parents the opportunity to speak the truth to each other is manifestly risible. Most children's interests will only be upheld if their parents don't divorce. In some cases, of course, intolerable conditions inside a marriage *will* make divorce sadly inevitable and even necessary. The problem is that what was once thought tolerable is now considered intolerable. The threshold of tolerability has been lowered in proportion to the elevation of individual happiness to dizzying and unreachable heights. Adult happiness, that is; because of course the price of the new adult tolerability threshold is the intolerable grief and disadvantage to which the children are then so often condemned. This grim picture is itself so intolerable that it has to be sanitised by 'informed' opinion, a process continued by Lord Pangloss's White Paper which perpetuates the fallacy that divorce can be achieved with the barest minimum of pain for all concerned. For some fortunate individuals, this may be the case; for the majority, particularly for the children, it is a cruel illusion.

The Abolition of Marriage

These proposals had their genesis in a different climate. The Law Commission report on which they are based was published in 1990, before the debate on the family got under way. It is less easy now to argue that divorce is intrinsically free of bad consequences for children. But among family lawyers, a distinctive nonjudgemental agenda has been running strongly for years, steadily eradicating the distinction between marriage and unmarriage through both statute and case law. In 1990, the perception that the practical application of law had diverged from statute led the distinguished family lawyer Brenda Hoggett, now Mrs Justice Hale, to write:

> Family law no longer makes any attempt to buttress the stability of marriage or any other union... Logically, we have already reached a point at which, rather than discussing which remedies should now be extended to the unmarried, we should be considering whether the legal institution of marriage continues to serve any useful purposes.[3]

Hoggett was a principal architect of the Law Commission's 1990 proposals on divorce.

There is no reason to think that Lord Mackay shares such a view. But he does think the divorce rate results from huge cultural pressures before which the law is powerless. On this analysis, all the law can hope to do is not make a bad situation worse. There is, of course, a glaring contradiction here because, while he says law can't mend marriages, he is creating a whole new structure of the twelve month delay and mediation to do precisely that. Clearly, the cultural primacy of individual choice and moral equivalence which fuels the divorce rate is not created by the law. But law embodies, imposes and reinforces the moral values of a society. Those values are currently amoral, hedonistic and pretend to be consequence-free. Are these really the values for which Lord Mackay wishes to be remembered?

Notes

1   Robertson, I., 'How Children Are Damaged By Divorce', *The Times*, 2 May 1995.

2   Cockett, M. and Tripp, J., *The Exeter Family Study*, University of Exeter Press, 1994.

3   Hoggett, B., 'Ends and Means: The Utility of Marriage as a Legal Institution', in Eekelaar, J.M., and Catz, S. (eds.), *Marriage and Cohabitation in Contemporary Societies*, Butterworth, 1980, p. 101.

Conflict and Divorce: Like a Horse and Carriage?

Patricia Morgan

T HE received wisdom is that there is nothing to be gained by hindering divorce, and much harm might be caused, since the threat to children stems primarily from conflict engendered by an unhappy marriage, and this will only be compounded by impediments to a speedy divorce.

Obviously, claims that divorce is best for the children when parents do not get on have been highly serviceable to reformers who would wish to emphasize the advantages of divorce and the perils of a continuing marriage. For years the established orthodoxy has been firmly against those who thought that homes must remain intact 'for the sake of the children'. However, in recent years it has become increasingly difficult to ignore or dismiss the overwhelming body of research which demonstrates that divorce both damages the parenting skills of the adults involved and has serious negative outcomes for children.

The Effect on Children

We now have a number of imposing studies, with very different methods and designs, providing a fairly comprehensive analysis of both children's experiences of divorce and its aftermath. Many consistently show greater difficulties in achieving educational and occupational goals, with poorer school work, more remedial provision, and lower academic attainment as well as poorer behaviour and adjustment. Even where some of the differences occur before homes break up, divorce widens the gap.[1]

The picture is repeated for law-breaking, where data from both the major British and American longitudinal studies of child development and delinquent careers show that boys who have been through marital breakdown and live with a lone parent or stepfather are generally twice as likely to be delinquent.[2]

The detrimental effects on health, behaviour and economic status are seen up to 30 years later. Almost half of Wallerstein and Kelly's subjects 'entered adulthood as worried, underachieving, self-deprecating, and sometimes angry young men and women'.[3] Sixty-per cent of this mainly middle-class sample were on a falling educational course compared to their fathers ten years after the divorce. At 18 and 21, young men from the 1946 British cohort study whose parents had divorced were three times more likely to be unemployed than those from intact families and even at 36, were twice as likely to be in the lowest income bracket. There was far less chance of going to university, passing examinations,[4] or getting qualifications.[5] With the pattern repeated for the 1958 cohort, men with fathers in non-manual occupations whose parents were divorced by the time they were 16 were more likely to end in unskilled occupations, even compared to those from intact manual working class families.[6]

The children of divorce are also predisposed to repeat patterns of marital disruption and single parenthood in their own lives, with daughters being far more likely to have teenage births, pre-marital births and failed marriages compared to girls who grew up in undisrupted homes.[7] For sons, divorce can be the first link in a chain of educational failure, early termination of training, poor mental or physical health, poor employment prospects, low marriageability and an increased chance of dropping out of the workforce entirely by the mid-30s.[8]

Parental role models, together with inadequate parental input and supervision, are likely to be important in accounting for children's future behaviour.[9] The stress and dissolution of the family at separation deprive the child of a supportive background and stable home base. In turn, involvement in sexual activities, gangs or peer groups is a general reaction to insubstantial domestic relationships and sparse home lives.

The Effect on Parents

Upon divorce, all aspects of parenting deteriorate as, just when children need extra help, the parents become preoccupied with their own concerns. Time does not necessarily bring improvement. While:

> ... many women in unhappy marriages assume that divorce will enable them to become happier, better mothers... In only a few families did the mother-child relationship in the postdivorce family surpass the quality of the relationship in the failing marriage ... the opposite occurred more frequently.[10]

Parents may want their child to 'grow up and be responsible' after divorce, shouldering a greater share of organisation in the family: *'The facts were they had to do more things for themselves'.*[11] This is especially so when the mother is courting or marrying again, with the adolescent pressurized to forego the usual help and guidance and achieve independence as quickly as possible. Parents who have more than one change of partner seem particularly liable to underestimate, or fail to see, their children's problems.[12]

Children from broken or incomplete families comprise a majority of the victims of all major forms of child abuse, including neglect.[13] Much of this is owed to the way that the father is often replaced at home by a succession of unrelated males.[14]

At the very least, children from previous unions easily become peripheral, if not inimical, to the relationship between the parent and her new mate. Moreover, parental care is costly in personal resources, and some people may be less than willing to use up time and money incurring such costs on unrelated young. Stepfathers are considerably less interested in children's school progress or employment prospects than fathers in unbroken families, as are divorced or remarried mothers, and both are more concerned to see that the children leave school early.[15]

As young men from step-families or with lone parents leave home for negative reasons at a rate three to five times higher than that for intact families,[16] so family breakdown and 'reconstituted families' are the foremost reasons for adolescent homelessness and receptions into institutional care.

Conflicting Opinions

The evidence that divorce is bad for children is now far less disputed then it has been until recently. However, advocates of divorce law reform still employ the argument that conflict in marriage does more damage and is to be avoided by making divorce easier. This view, which tends to be accepted without serious challenge, deserves close examination. Unfortunately, changes in family law tend to proceed largely or wholly independently of evidence.

☐ Firstly, we need to establish the extent to which divorce is precipitated by conflict in the marriage. Moreover, if there is conflict, what is its nature and are the children aware of it?

☐ Secondly, what role does conflict play in adverse outcomes for children?

☐ Thirdly, we need to consider the extent to which the availability of easy and cheap divorce actually causes what might have been minor or resolvable problems into major disputes—raising both the sum and intensity of conflict, *as well as* marital breakdown.

☐ Finally, we have to consider whether divorce can be said to represent the end of conflict for the children of that relationship, or whether conflict continues, or takes new forms or embroils further relationships and other people.

Does Conflict Cause Divorce?

In spite of the emphasis which divorce law reform advocates place on conflict in marriage, divorce often seems to have little or nothing to do with marital incompatibility, let alone open conflict. Wallerstein and Kelly could only characterise one third of divorces they studied as rationally undertaken to undo an unhappy marriage which was unlikely to change.[17] In just over half of the cases in the Exeter study there was no remembrance of major rows (involving leaving the house, throwing things or violence) recalled before the separation got under way.[18]

Divorce may be triggered by stressful experiences which have nothing to do with the marriage, like an unexpected death, an accident, or the sudden onset of psychiatric illness.[19] Others are resorted to out of anger, jealousy or to get attention, to punish the other spouse, because of boredom with being married or a feeling of having missed out as a single. Doctors, therapists or social workers may convince their clients that marriage is a hindrance to their freedom and development, or that they have been maltreated in some way. Those who consult solicitors over marital difficulties may be precipitated into legal proceedings when, due to a lack of guidelines, they are simply uncertain about what is tolerable, or whether their marriage has ended or not. An increasing number of separations seem to be occurring as a result of vague notions of incompatibility or simply the wish of one party for a relationship with someone else.

Demographer John Ermisch gives an important role to the relaxation of divorce law in the escalation of family breakdown, because this has encouraged the use of marriage as a base from which to go on searching for a better match or other opportunities.[20] Having altered the nature of the contract it terminates, permissive divorce has made all marriages provisional, and put them on a makeshift footing. People are under less pressure to restrain, resolve or conceal their disagreements, misdemeanours and complaints. In turn, the increasing divorce rate means greater familiarity with divorce as a solution to marital problems, and more willingness to use it. Moreover, as marriage has lost its power to bind future behaviour, people are dissuaded from investing in a common enterprise since they might lose out at separation.

As the grass is unlikely to be always greener in the next field, it is perhaps not all that surprising that surveys from both sides of the Atlantic indicate that as many as 50 per cent of men and at least 25 per cent of women feel later that divorce was the wrong decision and wish that they were still married.

Incentives to Divorce

There is nothing new about stress within marriage, or human discontent, dissatisfaction, emotional disturbance, petulance or opportunism. But the availability of unilateral divorce on demand means that there are no barriers to their translation into marital dissolution, or impediments to the freedom to respond to the apparent advantages and disadvantages of different options. As divorce has ceased to be a daunting process, requiring the establishment of an objectively defined fault of marital behaviour, the onus has shifted onto individuals to decide if their marriages have ended, knowing that there is easy access to cheap and approved ways of splitting up. Whatever the status of their grievances, if any, the instigators of divorce need incur little or no loss, and may even benefit. Men's unemployment, job instability and falling earnings significantly raise the chances of divorce. Since women almost invariably retain the home and children, and the benefits system is heavily skewed in favour of lone parents, there are strong incentives to dispose of husbands who have become economic liabilities, and the law readily provides the means to do it.[21] The MP Frank Field relates how:

> A number of women workers told me that thanks to family income supplement (now replaced by family credit) and more

generous housing rebates ... they had got rid of the 'jerk' to whom they had been married.

Many of these women ... begun their families in fairly conventional circumstances. But now, ten years or more later, they preferred to go it alone. The break-up agreement was that the man would leave, no maintenance would be demanded, but in return, the leaving had to be complete, with fathers having no continuing access to the children. All the women I spoke to that day expressed satisfaction with the arrangement. The children were not there to ask whether they viewed events so calmly.[22]

Does Divorce Free Children from Conflict?

Certainly, domestic discord is associated with problems in children, and some studies show behavioural difficulties in the children of high conflict families before any marital breakdown occurs,[23] but much seems to depend on whether there is open conflict, or if it embroils and distresses the children. The Hetherington team found that young children are more upset at the time of separation and over the following year than children in conflict ridden families, with aggressive behaviour, disruptive effects on school work, insecurity and lack of control at home and school, particularly for boys. This is in line with the observations of Wallerstein and Kelly who also found the deterioration in both behaviour and school performance affecting half of their older subjects. After two years the problems of Hetherington's separated children had fallen below those in high conflict families, but were still marked, along with a deterioration in intellectual functioning. But while problems increased with the period of conflict in intact marriages, a reduction of conflict led to improvement, without a divorce.

However, in the Exeter study the outcomes for children in intact families with high conflict more closely resembled those for children in other intact families than those broken by divorce. When children were living in intact families marked by discord between the parents the outcomes were intermediate between those of children in families with low reported conflict and lone-parent or step-families. Children of separated parents:

... were more likely to have encountered health problems (especially psychosomatic disorders), to have needed extra help at school, to have experienced friendship difficulties and to suffer from low self-esteem. These difficulties were highly significant, whether the comparisons were for individual questions or areas, for total scores in each area or for aggregate scores across all five. Statistically, the odds ratios from comparing matched pairs were mostly from two to six fold, and were never below unity.

Multivariate analysis confirmed that living in a re-ordered family, as opposed to an intact family, was the most significant association with poorer outcomes for children.[24]

Outcomes for children who had been through multiple disruptions were significantly poorer than for (first time) lone-parent or step-families. This parallels the results from Oregon of investigation into the direct and cumulative relationships between boys' behavioural problems and the family transitions they had been through.[25] It must be seen in relation to the current trend for 50 per cent of step-children to go through another family breakdown.

Clearly, family disruption is generally indicative of much instability, disorientation and inter-personal conflict. Not only are the suicide rates of both adults and children highly correlated with the divorce rate,[26] but the divorced of both sexes have higher death rates at all ages compared to the married, higher consulting levels for physical illness, mental disorders and accidents, and higher levels of admission to mental hospitals.[27] This must impair their ability to function properly as parents. In a recent study at Utah University the middle class divorced mothers and their children were significantly worse off than married mothers and their children on all measures of stress and psycho-social functioning. Whether they worked or not, there was lower well-being, more stress and less supportive behaviour in dealing with the children, who in turn had more behavioural problems.[28] The risk of unemployment rises for divorced men, and the 33 year-olds in the National Child Development Study were six times more likely to be economically inactive and over twice as likely to be unemployed compared to the married, and to derive all their income from state benefits.[29]

Wallerstein and Kelly found that 31 per cent of men and 42 per cent of women in their study had not achieved social or psychological stability even five years later. Not everyone is capable or well placed to 'reconstruct a happy life following divorce', particularly as it is marriage that brings order and security to many people's lives, and 'the structure itself provides their *raison d'etre* and their highest point of adult adjustment'.[30]

Does Divorce Increase Conflict?

Once the divorce process is under way it is highly likely to produce or exacerbate conflict even where this hardly, or never, existed before. Relationships between spouses are likely to deteriorate spectacularly and it is often at this point that all:

> ... the mutual ties that served sometimes to restrain the expression of hostility during the marriage are broken. Agitated...the partners to divorce often finish off whatever last vestiges of good feeling might have been left in the marriage.[31]

Wallerstein and Kelly report how over half of the children in their study now witnessed parental violence when, before this time, 75 per cent had never seen physical assault at home. Unfortunately, violence in the context of family breakdown seems to be especially remembered and to have a particularly damaging long term effect on development: '... an alarmingly high number of the children of divorce who witnessed family violence—two in five—repeated abuse in their own relationships'.[32] Similarly, in the Exeter study, while conflict and violence were more frequent in pre-divorce relationships: '... it was clear that these had often been made worse, or even begun, at the time when one or other party decided to separate'.[33]

Reformers have always assumed that easier divorce, enabling people to shed unwanted or abusive spouses, must mean less domestic violence, including murder and suicide. However, it is not only the threat to the safety of children from the increasing presence of stepfathers, boyfriends, and other unrelated, often transient, males in the home which suggests that the opposite may be true. Another type of domestic violence which has emerged involves the former husband. Some men may have been violent before separation. For others, the actual or threatened loss of their home, children, and sense of purpose—especially when it is involuntary—is highly destabilising.

Very recent examples include a man who killed his five-times married wife after she had taunted him with losing her and the home because he was not so sexy as a pop star she had never met. A husband killed the wrong man when he burst into his estranged wife's bedroom, which had been lent to another couple. A young father burnt himself and his two little children to death after being divorced. Then there was the redundant husband who went away to give his wife the 'time and space' she asked for.

She put this to use having an affair, and he was welcomed home by his children saying 'Daddy, I'm going to have a new brother and sister'. So he started a fire which badly burned his wife and a policeman.

Divorce often summons intense rage, rooted in the sense of being betrayed, exploited and humiliated. Furthermore, when marriages break up, a person's identity, along with all that they have built up over the years, is threatened. 'These feelings, and the internal conflicts they arouse, are not amenable to a quick fix or short recuperation',[34] in spite of the naïve hope that you can 'take the sting out of divorce' with counselling or mediation services which sort out the practical arrangements.

The Fantasy of 'No Fault' Divorce

In the divorce reformers' world nobody is responsible and there is no right and wrong. In the real world justice matters and people see each other as responsible agents and 'do not forget that divorce is rarely a mutual decision or that it is a voluntary act'. Wallerstein and Blakeslee comment that they have 'yet to meet one man, woman, or child who emotionally accepts "no fault" divorce', and that there is usually one who only goes along with it reluctantly or opposes.[35]

Conflict is particularly likely to arise as a direct result of the decision to separate in cases where the divorce is being unilaterally pursued for self-interested reasons that have little or nothing to do with the objective state of the marriage or the conduct of the other party.[36] These are, of course, precisely the kind of actions permitted by divorce-on-demand procedures.

Not only are few children relieved that their parents separate, but far less recall conflict in the marriage, or attach any significance to it, than is suggested by received wisdom. In Ann Mitchell's study,[37] as with a number of previous samples, three-quarters of the children recalled that their family life had been happy before the breakup; they did not necessarily equate conflict with an unhappy family life and certainly did not consider parental disagreements to be grounds for ending marriages.[38] Only one in five said that the marriage was the most difficult time. Half the children did not remember any parental conflict before separation, and those who did still did not think this a sufficient reason for parents to part: 'I know my parents argued and tried not to in front of me, but I'd not expected them to split'.[39] Similarly, Wallerstein and Kelly found hardly any pleased or relieved about the divorce, even if widespread or severe conflict existed in their families.

Insecurity for Children

The misery of children caught up in divorce centres as much or more on the departure of one parent as the conflict. Young children tend to blame themselves for this loss, and to worry that, if one parent has gone, then so might the other, or they are frightened of being sent away. J.S. Wallerstein and J.B. Kelly found that the aggression and fears of many were actually worse a year later, even if open conflict was not present in the divorces. However, even a quarter of those over nine worried about being abandoned and forgotten, particularly as the parents become preoccupied with their own concerns. Anger and hostility towards the parent or parents whom the adolescent believes initiated a breakup for which there appears to be no justification increase with age.

If children generally experience their parents' separation with disbelief, so they express wishes and entertain fantasies about reconciliation. Over half in Mitchell's sample had wanted reconciliation at some time, whether they imagined it possible or not, and one in six still wished that their parents could be reunited even many years later—often after one or both had remarried. Some 'children in the Exeter study had tried to involve their parents in joint Christmas and birthday celebrations, which proved disastrous'.[40] Over a third of the children in Wallerstein and Kelly's study were still intensely unhappy, depressed and dissatisfied with their lives five years after separation. With 56 per cent still finding no improvement over the pre-divorce family, less than a quarter were now relieved that their parents had parted.

Family disruption may continue, due to the way that parental care is not only undermined by a parent coping alone and establishing further relationships, but by continuing feuds with the ex-spouse. Wallerstein and Blakeslee admit that: 'The illusion we had held' at the start of their research 'that divorce brings an end to marital conflict—was shattered'. A third of the children were still party to intense bitterness between the parents five years or more later.[41] The assumption that parental conflict will cease at divorce is not only invalid; divorce itself *instigates conflict* which continues into the post-divorce period.[42] Thus, while the Exeter researchers found that only 7 of the 34 divorced families who experienced high conflict before separation avoided major rows afterwards, 21 out of the 41 who had only 'normal' rows during their marriage also had major conflict *after* separation.

> From the child's perspective conflict associated with parental separation, was ... reduced in 7 families ... increased or continued in 49 though subsequently reduced over time in 15 of these. In 17 families continuing conflict had resulted in loss of regular contact for the child.[43]

Only four out of ten separated parents in this study found it possible to talk to each other about arrangements for the children without fear, anger, resentment and frustration. It is commonly observed that vindictive custodial parents often find all manner of reasons to reduce or stop the father's visits. In 1965 nearly half of the divorced mothers interviewed by W.J. Goode[44] wanted their children to have less access to fathers or none at all. Twenty years on, we find only a quarter of Mitchell's custodial parents expressing any positive attitude towards their children keeping in touch with the absent parent, and a quarter wanted to terminate all access. (Most of these had succeeded.)

The children cannot easily remain on the sidelines of parental conflict, as they might during a marriage. They are both the focus of disputes and recruited into hostilities.

> It follows that separation and divorce do not necessarily reduce damaging conflict and, indeed, that as a generality the reverse may be true. In other words, the experience of most children whose parents divorce is of *increased* conflict over an extended period, with the child involved to an extent that may not have been the case while the marriage lasted.[45]

Moreover, the resident parent's changing relationships are bound to multiply the occasions for emotional crises and domestic disputes, exposing children to more conflict and stress. In turn, parent-child conflict is also higher in broken families. Typically, in the Exeter study, there were more major disagreements between children and parents in lone-parent and step-families

than in intact families—even intact families where conflict levels
were high.

Conflict in Broken Families

Conflict in broken families is not only more likely to occur than
in intact families, but may be more damaging than high levels
of conflict in married families, especially for boys. In two parent
homes, the second parent often provides a corrective influence
and balance in disputes, which compensates for the disorientating
effects of domestic conflict or poor relations between the child
and one parent.[46] In turn, children who have a good relationship
with one parent are less likely to have problems than where
there are poor relations with both parents.

A good paternal relationship for children of divorced parents
is beneficial, yet around 25 per cent of children lose contact with
their father soon after parental separation and, over the longer
term, this rises to a half.[47] When contact exists, this may not be
regular, let alone frequent. Even when the post-divorce involvement of non-residential parents is high, there is still a steady
decline in contact over time. The ending of the relationship with
the father is hastened by the re-partnering of either parent. This
is doubly unfortunate, since this may not only entail the further
marginalisation of children from previous marriages, but a child
is likely to have less trouble adjusting to the new partner if he
has a good relationship with the non-resident parent.

The Myth of the Re-constituted Family

For a child, the post-divorce situation is likely to be benign to
the degree that parent-child relationships can be maintained at
the level which existed in the pre-divorce family or, if there were
difficulties, to the extent that these can be improved upon. Such
an ideal divorce must recreate something like the child-rearing
conditions of the harmonious, intact home. In the circumstances
it is a tall order, and one which militates against the whole
rationale and dynamic of divorce. It is marriage which is
designed to facilitate what divorce is made to thwart, the child's
continuous access to two people for whom his welfare is their
joint and paramount concern, and for whom the children are
part of, rather than extraneous or burdensome to, their current
aspirations and concerns.

The 10 to 20 per cent of children, whom studies generally show to be actually relieved or to have benefited after their parents have separated, have invariably got away from rejecting, insane, abusive, or otherwise destructive parents. Here the parent-child tie is already absent or abrogated. Otherwise, for most children, there are really no such things as second or reconstituted families. Their own parents are irreplaceable and their marriage is therefore indissoluble. They 'do not perceive divorce as a second chance ... They feel that their childhood has been lost forever'.[48] Human young need their parents far longer than any other species and 'children are tragically aware of this fact'.[49] Upon divorce they lose:

> ... something that is fundamental to their development—the family structure. The family comprises the scaffolding upon which children mount successive developmental stages, from infancy into adolescence. It supports their psychological, physical and emotional ascent into maturity. ... Whatever its shortcomings, children perceive the family as the entity that provides the support and protection that they need.[50]

Any mammal species in which the parent and offspring lacked the imperative to cleave to each other would have poor chances of survival and success. Human beings need an elaborate process of socialisation and education to re-equip each generation, and this is inseparable from the existence of morally and legally validated institutions of kinship and marriage. Fatherhood and motherhood are relationships of personal commitment, where the moral imperatives of kinship involve binding mutual interdependence and willingness to forego selfish gratification for the sake of others.

Divorce the Great Destroyer

Laws, norms and rules that reflected the interests of society at large in maintaining cohesion, continuity and the sources of mutual trust were traditionally brought to bear on sexual and reproductive behaviour. Family law stressed the preservation of the marriage bond, taking the view that people have good and bad impulses, and that it is a function of the law to strengthen the good and control the bad.

As the law now stands it does not protect the vulnerable and curb the unscrupulous, but allies itself with the spouses who want to break up marriages. In so doing, it rewards selfishness, egoism and destructiveness over altruistic commitment. This will be even more obviously the case under Lord Mackay's proposed reforms.

Without a firm legal framework to maximise the chances of peaceful and harmonious homes, domestic insecurity and instability will increase. It is divorce itself, or the de-institution-alisation of marriage, which is the problem. Divorce is a great destroyer that is eating the heart out of society as well as savaging children's lives. Its depredations will not be reversed given ever so many mediators, or conciliators. This reversal will only happen when marriage is restored as a distinct legal status based on serious and permanent mutual commitment by a man and a woman, recognised and supported by the state.

Notes

1   Crellin, E., *Growing Up in a One Parent Family: a Long-term Study of Child Development*, Slough: NFER, 1976; Essen, J., 'Living in One Parent Families: Attainment at School', *Child: Care, Health and Development*, 1979, Vol. 5, pp. 189-200; Burghes, L., *Lone Parenthood and Family Disruption*, Occasional Paper 18, London: Family Policy Studies Centre, 1994. Dawson, D.A., *Family Structure and Children's Health: United States 1988*, Series 10:178 Vital and Health Statistics, Maryland: US Department of Health and Human Services, 1991 and Allison, P.D., Furstenberg, F.F., 'How Marital Dissolution Affects Children', *Developmental Psychology*, 1989, Vol. 25, pp. 540-49.

2   West, D.J. and Farrington, D.P., *Who Becomes Delinquent?*, Heinemann, 1973; and *The Delinquent Way of Life*, Heinemann, 1977. Ferri, E., *Step Children*, NFER-Nelson, 1984. West, D.J., *Delinquency: Its Roots, Careers and Prospects*, Heinemann, 1982. Capaldi, D.D. and Patterson, G.R., 'Relations of Parental Transitions to Boys' Adjustment Problems: i. A Linear Hypothesis, ii: Mothers at Risk for Transitions and Unskilled Parenting', *Developmental Psychology*, Vol. 27, No. 3, 1991, pp. 489-504.

3   Wallerstein, J.S. and Blakeslee, S., *Second Chances*, New York: Ticknor and Fields, p. 299.

4   Maclean, M., and Wadsworth, M.E.J., *The Interests of Children after Parental Divorce*, Centre for Socio-Legal Studies, Wolfson College, Oxford: Oxford University Press, 1988; and abstract in *The International Journal of Law and the Family*, Vol. 2, 1988, pp. 155-66; Elliott, B.J. and Richards, M.P.M., 'Children and Divorce: Educational Performance and Behaviour Before and After Parental Separation', *International Journal of Law and the Family*, 1991, pp. 258-276; and 'Parental Divorce and the Life Chances of Children', *Family Law*, November 1991.

5   Kuh, D. and Maclean, M., 'Women's Childhood Experiences of Parental Separation and their Subsequent Health and Status in Adulthood', *Journal of Biosocial Science*, Vol. 22, pp. 121-35.

6   Elliot, B.J. and Richards, M.P.M., *op. cit.*

7   McLanahan, S., 'Family Structure and Dependency: Early Transitions to Female Household Headship', *Demography*, Vol. 25, No. 1, 1988, pp. 1-17; 'The Consequences of Single Parenthood for Subsequent Generations', *Focus*, Institute for Research on Poverty, University of Winconsin-Madison; also with Bumpass, L., 'Intergenerational Consequences of Family disruption', *American Journal of Sociology*, Vol. 94, No.1, 1988, pp. 130-152; Kiernan, K.E., 'The Impact of Family Disruption in Childhood on Transitions Made in Young Adult Life', *Population Studies*, Vol. 46, 1992; Keith, V.M. and Finlay, B., 'The Impact of Parental Divorce on Children's Educational Attainment, Marital Timing and Likelihood of Divorce', *Journal of Marriage and the Family*, Vol. 50, 1988, pp. 797-809; Millar, B.C. and Moore, M.A., 'Adolescent Sexual Behaviour, Pregnancy and Parenting: Research Through the 1980s', *Journal of Marriage and the Family*, Vol. 53, 1991, p. 1,028.

8   Maclean, M. and Wadsworth, M.E.J., *op. cit.*

9   Dornbusch, S.M. *et al.*, 'Single Parents, Extended Households and the Control of Adolescents', *Child Development*, Vol. 56, 1985, pp. 326-41; Flewelling, R.L. and Bauman, K.E., 'Family Structure as a Predictor of Initial Substance Use and Sexual Intercourse in Early Adolescence', *Journal of Marriage and the Family*, Vol. 52, 1990, pp. 171-81; Hoffman, J.P., 'Investigating the Age Effects of Family Structure on Adolescent Marijuana Use', *Journal of Youth and Adolescence*, Vol. 23, 1994, pp. 215-232.

10 Wallerstein and Blakeslee, *op. cit.*, p. 187.

11 Cockett and Tripp, *op. cit.*, p. 30.

12 Cockett and Tripp, *ibid.*, p. 35.

13 Gartner, R., 'Family Structure, Welfare Spending, and Child Homicide in Developed Democracies', *Journal of Marriage and the Family,* Vol. 53, 1991, pp. 231-240; Whelan, R., *Broken Homes and Battered Children,* Oxford: Family Education Trust, 1994; Gordon, M. and Creighton, S.J., 'Natal and Non-Natal Fathers as Sexual Abusers in the United Kingdom: A Comparative Analysis', *Journal of Marriage and the Family,* Vol. 50, 1988, pp. 99-105.

14 see Whelan, R., *op. cit.*

15 Ferri, E., *op. cit.*

16 Kiernan, K., 'The Impact of Family Disruption in Childhood on Transitions Made in Young Adult Life', *Population Studies,* Vol. 46, 1992, pp. 213-34.

17 Wallerstein and Blakeslee, *op. cit.*

18 Cockett and Tripp, *op. cit.*

19 Wallerstein, J.S. and Kelly, J.B., *Surviving the Breakup: How Children and Parents Cope with Divorce,* Grant McIntyre, 1978, p. 20.

20 Ermisch, J., *Lone Parenthood,* Cambridge University Press, 1991.

21 see Morgan, P., *Farewell to the Family?,* London: Institute of Economic Affairs, Health and Welfare Unit, 1995.

22 Field, F., *Making Welfare Work: Reconstructing Welfare for the Millennium,* Institute of Community Studies, 1995.

23 Block, J.H. *et al.,* 'The Personality of Children Prior to Divorce: A Prospective Study', *Child Development,* Vol. 57, 1986, pp. 827-40; Smith, M.A. and Jenkins, J.M., 'The Effects of Marital Disharmony on Prepubertal Children', *Journal of Abnormal Child Psychology,* Vol. 19, 1991, pp. 625-44.

24 Cockett and Tripp, *op. cit.,* p. 35.

25 Capaldi, D.M. and Patterson, G.R., 'Relations of Parental Transitions to Boys' Adjustment Problems: I, A Linear Hypothesis. II, Mothers at Risk for Transitions and Unskilled Parenting', *Developmental Psychology,* Vol. 27930, 1991, pp. 489-504.

26 Breault, K.D., 'Suicide in America: The Test of Durkheim's Theory of Religious and Family Integration, 1933-1980', *American Journal of Sociology,* Vol. 92, 1986, pp. 651-52. Stack, S., 'The Impact of Divorce on Suicide in Norway, 1951-1980', *Journal of Marriage and the Family,* Vol. 51, 1989, pp. 229-38; and 'The Effect of Suicide in Denmark, 1961-1980', *The Sociological Quarterly,* Vol. 31, 1990, pp. 361-68.

27 Dominian, J. *et al.*, *Marital Breakdown and the Health of the Nation,* London: One Plus One, 1991.

28 Pet, M.A., Vaughan-Cole, B. and Wampold, B.E., 'Maternal Employment and Perceived Stress: Their Impact on Children's Adjustment and Mother/Child Interaction in Young Divorced and Married Families', *Family Relations,* Vol. 43, 1994, pp. 151-58.

29 Ferri, E., *Life at 33,* National Children's Bureau, 1993.

30 Wallerstein and Blakeslee, *op. cit.,* p. 53.

31 *Ibid,* p. 26.

32 Wallerstein and Blakeslee, *op. cit.,* p. 121.

33 Cockett and Tripp, *op. cit.,* p. 36.

34 Wallerstein and Blakeslee, *op. cit.,* pp. 6-7.

35 *Ibid,* and p. 39.

36 Cockett and Tripp, *op. cit.*

37 Mitchell, A., *Children in the Middle,* London: Tavistock, 1985.

38 Landis, J.T., 'The Trauma of Children When Parents Divorce', *Marriage and Family Living,* Vol. 22, 1960, pp. 7-22; and Walczck,Y. and Burns, S., *Divorce: the Child's Point of View,* Harper & Row, 1984.

39 *Ibid,* p. 103.

40 Cockett and Tripp, *op. cit.,* p. 57.

41 Wallerstein and Blakeslee, *op. cit.,* p. xviii.

42 Cockett and Tripp, *op. cit.,* p. 36.

43 Cockett and Tripp, *op. cit.,* p. 43.

44 Goode, W.J., *Women in Divorce,* Free Press, 1965.

45 Cockett and Tripp, *op. cit.,* p. 58.

46 Richards, M.P. and Dyson, M., *Separation, Divorce and the Development of Children,* Cambridge Child Care and Development Group, 1982.

47 Mitchell, A., *Someone to Turn To: Experiences of Help before Divorce,* Aberdeen University Press, 1981.

48 Wallerstein and Blakeslee, *op. cit.,* p. 14.

49 *Ibid,* p. 12.

50 *Ibid,* pp. 11-12.

Justice and Liberty in Marriage and Divorce

Norman Barry

I N England and Wales there are over 160,000 divorces a year, over a third of current marriages can be expected to end in divorce, with higher failure rates for remarriages, and one in five children under the age of 16 have experienced divorce in their families. In addition, one in three children is now born out of wedlock (though often of 'stable relationships'). In some parts of the Western world the figures are, if anything, slightly worse. In the US one in two marriages can be expected to fail, with similarly declining longevity of remarriages. Australia which has had perhaps the most lax (I do not use the word 'liberal', for reasons which will become apparent) divorce laws in the West since 1975 has experienced similar rises in marital breakdown. The emergence of single-parent families, either as a consequence of divorce or from the attractions of unmarried motherhood, has disturbed policy-makers.

One reason is purely economic: the alarming increase in welfare costs brought about by the decline in the traditional family unit. The autonomy and self-sufficiency of this form of living, which is essential for the sustaining of a free society of independent individuals and families, is obviously threatened by the inexorable rise in single-parent households: the annual costs of which have risen to a staggering £9 billion. This phenomenon has been caused by both the increase in unmarried motherhood and the costs associated with the increase in divorce (largely due to both the inadequacy of maintenance payments and the failure to enforce them). The costs, however, are not simply measurable in terms of state welfare spending. Many critics[1] now maintain that the decay in social morality that we are witnessing and the corroding of traditional institutions have much wider, though related, implications. Some have to do with long-term economic considerations and focus on the fact that economic prosperity in the West (and elsewhere) has been associated with the stable family unit. Others are concerned more directly with moral issues, most noticeably the decline in personal responsibility for action which is said to have been brought about by permissive family and divorce laws.

There is, however, an additional moral question which is likely to become increasingly more pressing: that is the justice of the divorce laws themselves. It is a common view that justice and fairness have no place in matrimonial matters; that the cold formalism that they represent is irrelevant, if not actually harmful, to the emotionally-charged atmosphere of divorce proceedings. This view would appear to be reflected in the development of matrimonial law in Western societies where notions of 'blame' and 'fault' have been almost eliminated not only from the question of the grounds for the dissolution of a marriage but, more importantly, from the terms of the 'ancillaries' or settlement itself, i.e. the arrangements for the custody of children and the division of property. Along with this is the tendency for 'conciliation' between potentially warring spouses to replace adversarial processes (which are traditionally concerned with the authoritative determination of right and wrong).

Attitudes to Marriage

It should be noted that marriage remains a popular arrangement although people are marrying at a slightly older age.[2] Even though in both Britain and America the chance of marital success will *decrease* with succeeding marriages the *idea* of permanent matrimonial union is as alluring as ever. Indeed, the well-attested phenomenon of divorced women re-marrying at a slightly lower rate than divorced men is surely better explained by economic factors, e.g. the fact that married women normally retain custodial rights over children reduces their attractiveness as potential partners (as does the fact, especially in America, of their reduced economic circumstances), than it is by any emotionally-based disinclination for the married state. All social surveys have clearly revealed that the household headed by a married couple remains people's ideal. However, their *behaviour* clearly belies this: indeed it indicates that formal marriage, with all its obligations and responsibilities, has become one of a range of choices of life-styles rather than an arrangement of over-whelming moral importance. This difference between what people profess to believe about marriage and how they actually behave is analogous to the case of citizens *expressing* a desire for expanded public services and a willingness to pay for them in higher taxes (as revealed in opinion surveys) *and* their reluctance to vote for governments to do precisely these things. Costless morality would seem to be a universal human desire.

Despite the evidence of public opinion surveys our attitudes to marriage have undoubtedly changed. The important question here is the explanation for this. What was once viewed as a binding commitment, to be enjoyed or endured, has tended to become a provisional agreement, to be terminated at the whim of both or either of two parties. Furthermore, its significance as an indissoluble union of a man and woman has increasingly come to be challenged: hence the demand for homosexual 'marriage', which has actually been acknowledged in some jurisdictions. Thus the solemnity of the marriage vow has been badly compromised by the ease with which its burdens can be repudiated and by the diminution of its special significance as a unique union between the sexes.

Whether the dramatic changes in marriage that we have witnessed represent a genuine change in the public perception of the institution, and in the force of the moral duties that it involves, or that changes in the divorce law (and in the distribution of costs and benefits that the dissolution of marriage involves) are more significant is a difficult question. However, it certainly cannot be denied that the passage of the 1969 Divorce Reform Act (and subsequent legislation) in Britain was a significant factor in the rapid increase in marital breakdown. An important point here (to be considered below) is not merely the *de facto* elimination of fault from the grounds of divorce itself but also its (almost, but not quite) removal from the conditions governing the post-divorce settlement. It is here that the demands of justice (scarcely honoured at all in current divorce law) may well compete with the desire for personal liberty. The evidence would seem to be that however 'moral' people would like to be with regard to marriage, the incentive structures facing couples are unlikely to encourage the preservation of that morality.

The facts of marital breakdown do suggest that there has been a change in the *meaning* of marriage in the contemporary world: a change that has been highlighted by the growth of a new spirit of liberty (at least in social matters): a belief that individuals should be the autonomous makers of their own lives, and should not be confined by traditional rules and practices, however advantageous these might be for social stability. This is no doubt partly a consequence of the greater participation of women in the workforce; a fact which must go some way towards explaining why it is that, in most Western countries, women are disproportionately the instigators of divorce proceedings. Any attempt to revert to traditional roles with regard to marriage would badly compromise the newly-won independence of women.

Marriage as a Vow

In the history of marriage we can see two competing concepts at work: marriage as a vow and as a contract. The connections between marriage and divorce on the one hand, and liberty and justice on the other cannot be understood without an understanding of vows and contracts.

To put it simply, a marriage vow is a binding and solemn commitment, under either canon or civil law. It is specifically addressed to the subjectivist notion of morality as a matter of personal choice, and, in relation to marriage, it presupposes that the permanent union of a man and woman represents a higher, objective ethic. It follows from this that no marriage can be revocable at the mere whim of the parties, even if there is mutual agreement between them, since the taking of a vow specifically precludes that subjectivity. The philosopher Hegel put the matter well in his claim that no moral community could be constructed out of the subjective choices of individuals alone (even when subject to law) and in his argument that a purely empirical conception of liberty (i.e. as the absence of constraint) is destructive of social order. A marriage vow imposes an unavoidable limitation on our desires for the purpose of achieving a higher organic union, which, in effect, releases the partners from the constraints of their merely ephemeral and subjective desires: 'their union is a self-restriction, but in fact it is their liberation because in it they attain their substantive self-consciousness'.[3] From this perspective, it is easy to see why Hegel should attach such importance to the wedding *ceremony*, for this symbolises the depth of the renunciation of subjective desire in the way that a formal agreement or contract never can.

This does not mean that a marriage may never be dissolved. Those who believe that marriage is a vow may admit to circumstances in which the union has become meaningless, so that the partners cannot achieve any objective morality by its continuation. But the important point here is that the decision as to whether these conditions are met ought not to be that of the partners, that would be to surrender to the caprice of subjectivism, but it should be the objective conclusion of a disinterested third party[4] (the Church or the state). The Catholic church goes further when it maintains that a marriage can never be dissolved but only annulled, i.e. deemed never to have been a 'marriage' in the proper sense of the word.

Before dismissing all this as a piece of heady, organic metaphysics which has no place in a largely individualistic Western world, in which such a high premium is placed on personal autonomy, it must be recognised that, in a confused way, the public does regard marriage, in theory at least, as representative of a form of union qualitatively different from a mere agreement or contract. If it is a contract it is *meant* to be a permanent one; almost as a kind of protection from the instability, and ephemeral nature of, private desires. Indeed, the well-attested fact that many people come to regret their divorces suggests that the relentless subjectivism of the modern liberal state may have destructive effects.[5] The fact that suicide rates, depression and alcoholism are much higher in divorced couples (leaving aside the adverse effects on children) further supports the view of cultural conservatives that individualism is a false god that punishes especially harshly those who choose to live by its tenets. At the very least, the onerous conditions imposed on individuals by the concept of marriage as a vow is a pointed reminder that morality does not come easily to individuals, that we may require something outside ourselves to help us to realise ourselves fully. This can only be more or less intransigent and restrictive law.

Marriage as a Contract

The rival conception of marriage as a contract between two parties which can ultimately be repudiated has, of course, come to dominate Western thought, principally because it is more consonant with individualism. It is, though, still recognised to be a special sort of contract, not directly analogous to commercial contracts. This is not merely because of the existence of children (relationships between parents and children, and the obligations involved here, surely cannot be subsumed under the notion of contract), it is also because 'society' still seems to accept that the emotional aspects of marriage prevent the problems associated with it from being resolved by the cold, formality of law. Marriage contracts are expected to be permanent and not to be repudiated at will, however much people's behaviour belies this.

As Ferdinand Mount observes in his history of the family,[6] the idea of marriage as a contract predates Christianity and is an enduring feature of civilised society. It is indeed consonant with many features of Christianity. According to Mount, the idea of marriage as an unbreakable vow was a kind of mutation out of original Christian thought. It was, in fact, an example of the capture of the individual by a church-state hierarchy and it condemned people to permanent misery by its rigorous condemnation and prevention of divorce. This tyranny was neither necessary to society, nor even Christianity, since all civilised societies have granted the right to divorce and to some form of compensation to injured parties should it occur. That divorce was not antithetical to sincere Christians is attested to by John Milton's famous polemic against repressive marriage laws.[7] His view stressed the essential *privacy* of love and marriage and he railed against the Church and the state for attempting to convert and distort the personal experiences of individuals for public purposes. The prohibition of divorce was simply an expression of *power*. In Milton's theory, wanton subjectivism is severely qualified by a commitment to legal procedures that would make appropriate, and predictable, arrangements for the victims of a dissolution of marriage.

The fact that the original theory of marriage as a contract was outrageously sexist, in that rarely were women given the right to terminate unilaterally a marriage, should not distract the modern reader from the basic point: that marriage must ultimately be understood in terms of the private satisfactions that it gives individuals; satisfactions which are not readily available outside the marital state. Thus, the marriage as a contract theory normally distinguishes marriage from a mere private arrangement between consenting adults. It is the *public*, and most often secular, recognition of the more or less permanent (but not necessarily irrevocable) nature of the marriage contract that distinguishes it from a mere commercial contract. No subjective choices, however intensely felt, can reproduce that particular public validation which distinguishes a marriage from two partners amicably living together. However, this concession to anti-individualism should not be understood as a retreat into the marriage as a vow theory; for the contract, however onerous, and however much it depends upon public validation, is still a product of private desires and its dissolution does not depend upon the intervention of third parties.

What it does have in common with ordinary commercial contracts is the idea of justice. A commercial contract is not irrevocable but when a contract is revoked the disappointment of legitimate expectations which that action involves justifies compensation. Breach of contract is a primary type of injustice. The predictability of a commercial order could not be guaranteed if compensation were not paid for breach of contract. It would indeed be meaningless. The theory of marriage as a contract involves a similar notion of justice, even though the personal and emotional commitments that marriage involves are perhaps not fully justiciable: feelings are clearly not exchangeable goods. Nevertheless, the kinds of investments that people make in marriage, in terms of property and the efforts involved in the nurturing of children, are comprehensible within a theory of justice that confines itself to procedural rules of equality and to appropriate forms of compensation for those 'victimised' by the breach of the basic features of the marital contract (though this may be extraordinarily difficult to demonstrate).

Historically, the theory of marriage as a contract has triumphed precisely because it meets with the rise of individualism and the secularisation of modern life. Like it or not, personal liberty and autonomy have become irresistible demands and to pretend otherwise (in law or morality) is simply to encourage hypocrisy. People will break their vows and the tolerance of such breaches will eventually lead to a degrading of the vow itself. An example may be seen in the most extreme form of the vow: the Catholic marriage which can only be annulled. All sorts of casuistry (and hypocrisy) have been used by Catholics anxious to end their marriages so that the concept of annulment has on occasions been simply degraded. What was or was not a genuine marriage turns on the subjective opinion of the Catholic hierarchy. Prominent Catholic public figures seem to have little difficulty in getting annulments. Indeed, during the debate in Ireland leading up to the (unsuccessful) referendum asking the

population whether they wished divorce to be permitted, some
devout Catholics actually said that it should because the ease
with which annulments could be obtained was itself making a
mockery of the idea of indissoluble marriage.

The Meaning of Marriage Today

The most obvious feature of marriage in Western societies is
that it is neither a vow nor a contract. Although people may
express a desire for the solemnity of a formal arrangement that
distinguishes it from an informal partnership terminable at will,
the latter is precisely what it has become. The most important
fact here is not merely the ease with which a marriage may be
dissolved but that the settlement normally bears no relationship
to the behaviour of the parties to the original contract. This is
a clear contrast with commercial law. Conduct has not only been
de facto eliminated as a ground for divorce but it also has little
relevance to decisions about the custody of children and the
division of property.

Obviously, the needs of children should be ranked higher than
the 'rights' of the partners (a necessary modification to the
theory of marriage as a contract) but there is no reason within
liberal theory why the contractual elements should be eliminated
elsewhere. Justice sometimes may have to give way to other
values in the marriage relationship but it does not follow at all
from correct liberal theory that it should be discarded entirely,
even though the law deals with the most sensitive and emotionally-charged aspects of our lives. It is a curious irony in
contemporary liberal social theory that it should on the one hand
demand the autonomy of individuals, and celebrate their rights
to realise themselves as rational agents, yet, on the other, it
permits a retreat into *sentimentality* in its analysis of perhaps
the most important choice, i.e. that of a marriage partner, that
individuals are likely to make.

It is strange, too, that justice, that most favoured of liberal
concepts, should have received so little attention in (with one
exception, to be considered below), and so little application to,
marriage. The lacuna in liberal theory here may partly be
because of the current concern for 'social' rather than procedural
justice.

Indeed, the current obsession with 'conciliation' as the method for resolving differences between partners is deliberately contrasted favourably with legal adjudication. Progressive thinkers would appear to prefer a form of social therapy to the authoritative determination of right and wrong. This has been taken to extremes in Australia which has perhaps the most permissive divorce law in the West (Family Law Act, 1975). There, Family Courts have virtually dispensed with formal notions of legality and have decided disputes between spouses on the vaguest and most indeterminate of grounds. This has naturally led to unpredictability; which is perhaps the most damaging shortcoming a legal system can have. In fact conciliation is a primitive rather than a progressive notion precisely because it dispenses with the ideas of right, wrong, and personal responsibility for action.

Marriage and Liberty

In Western countries the law regarding marriage has become extremely permissive, perhaps more so than individuals would like. In particular, it has brought about a perversion of the moral ideal of liberty. Originally, the moral right to liberty was based upon the notion of personal responsibility for action. Individuals are treated as free agents capable of making rational choices because of their awareness of, and responsibility for, the consequences of their choices. In traditional liberal theory a person's moral development is very largely a function of a learning process in which he or she has to pay the costs of the mistakes that so often flow from the exercise of freedom. In theory, the idea of a society based on contract is not at all permissive precisely because contracts are onerous; they place burdens on the parties which they cannot easily cast aside. Liberty consists in the fact that contracts are freely made. Of course, free choice and personal responsibility are not limited to contracts but include any form of voluntary action in which costs can be more or less known. However, in modern Western society the state has gradually absorbed the costs that accrue when individuals make mistakes. Hence the rise of the one-parent families, the increase in marital breakdown and other undesirable social phenomena which are encouraged by permissive laws and easily-available welfare.

Good Intentions and British Law

The noticeable fact in all this is that the gradual disintegration
of personal responsibility began with good intentions, which
would have been approved of by John Milton. Prior to 1969
many married couples in Britain were trapped in unhappy
marriages which presumably were of little benefit to their
children, let alone themselves. The necessity of proving a marital
offence to secure a divorce meant that couples who would have
voluntarily agreed to separate had either to endure their misery
or engage in collusive activity (which itself brought about
disrespect for the law). However, the terms of the divorce
settlement were directly related to the conduct that led to the
divorce so that at least a strong concept of personal responsibility for action remained.

The 1969 Act,[8] by introducing the concept of the 'irretrievable
breakdown' of a marriage (although it did not entirely remove
the notion of fault or conduct) at least opened the way for a
more civilised and less hypocritical approach to divorce. There
are now five possible conditions for the demonstration of irretrievable breakdown: mutual agreement after a two-year separation, adultery, unreasonable behaviour, desertion for at least two
years and unilateral renunciation of the marriage after a five-
year separation. Of course there is still some chicanery involved
if couples require a 'quickie' divorce since then one of the fault-
based reasons for irretrievable breakdown has to be invoked.

Courts have been remarkably lax in their interpretation of
unreasonable behaviour (which has to be sufficiently objectionable
to make it impossible for the petitioner to live with his or her
spouse). Although the courts have the authority to refuse to
grant a divorce even when the petition is undefended, this is
rarely exercised. They have not regarded it as their duty to
protect the sanctity of marriage even when the complaint might
be regarded as trivial. Thus we do have *de facto* divorce on
demand in this country.

Lawyers have worried about some of the legal processes
involved in all this but for conservatives this is not the real
problem. The connection between liberty and personal responsibility was broken through developments in the common law, which
were later embodied in statute. The key case is *Wachtel v.
Wachtel* (1973)[9] in which it was ruled by the judges at both the

lower court and on appeal that conduct should not normally be relevant to the ancillaries. Echoing the prevailing 'liberal' sentiment, Lord Denning, the Master of the Rolls, wrote that 'the court should not reduce its order for financial provision merely because of what was formerly regarded as guilt or blame. To do so would be to impose a fine for supposed misbehaviour in the course of an unhappy married life'.[10] The courts officially declared their incompetence to penetrate the secrets of a marriage in order to attribute blame or to allocate responsibility for its failure. With the qualification that, except where it is 'both obvious and gross', conduct should not be taken into account, the courts, under the precedent established under *Wachtel*, were led to ignore questions of right and wrong, justice and injustice. Under later statute law,[11] conduct which is so gross that not to consider it would be 'inequitable' is supposed to be relevant but this provision appears towards the end of a list of facts appropriate to the ancillaries. It has rarely been invoked.

It is then quite inaccurate to describe marriage as a contract since no adverse consequences are visited upon those who breach its terms. Again, it is impossible to describe the freedoms that legal changes have introduced as emanations out of traditional liberal or conservative doctrine since the new liberties are almost completely detached from any notion of personal responsibility for action. Thus, although it is true that some conservatives[12] have blamed the rise of permissiveness, the disintegration of the family and the devaluation of the institution of marriage on the rise of a contract-based society and individualistic order devoid of communal, moral obligations, their argument misrepresents the traditional liberal position. A contract-based society is not amoral or uncontrollably egoistic even though the duties that character- ise it are largely self-assumed. The changes in matrimonial law, both in common law and statute, that have occurred were specifically designed to remove the notion of moral responsibility for action in marriage. It is, then, the institutions of the state that have been the trail-blazers in the rise of permissiveness.

Divorce, Permissiveness and the Law

Britain has been little different from the rest of the world in the eagerness of its legislators and judges to remove justice and personal responsibility from matrimonial law. However, it may be doubted that these innovations represent a genuine change in public opinion with regard to moral conduct. One suspects that the taste for adultery and other forms of marital misconduct is pretty much constant over time. What has changed, however, is the incentive structure that now faces potentially erring spouses. One does not have to be a soulless economic determinist to suggest that costs and benefits have an influence on human behaviour. It is naïve to argue that proper moral conduct can be sustained without a legal framework that at least sets the terms for that conduct.

There are, of course, other reasons than legal changes which can explain the rise in the divorce rate.[13] The increase in the employment of women undoubtedly makes a difference to the economics of the household since it alters the division of labour between the partners: the wife is no longer confined to performing household tasks and the husband is not the sole generator of income. Thus the familiar 'gains from trade' that accrue from marriage are less readily available. Again, one would expect lower divorce rates among married couples with children than those without since the latter have not normally accumulated valuable marital 'capital' which is worth preserving. The fact that divorce is more likely within the first five years of marriage than later hardly requires explanation. All these propositions are well-established, and the behaviour they describe is affected by changes in the external constraints that are faced by married couples. However, similar accurate predictions could be made about the behaviour of couples who were not actually married but living together.

The issue that concerns most critical observers of contemporary marriage is primarily moral: it is about the changing status of marriage as a valuable *social* institution that has been generated by the familiar legal innovations. I would suggest that the only way in which marriage can be resuscitated is by reincorporating the idea of justice into its fundamental features. The difficulty is that there is now much disagreement about what justice in marriage means.

Justice, Contracts and Marriage

Justice is relevant to marriage in two distinct but nevertheless inter-related ways. First, the relaxation of the conditions attending divorce has undoubtedly created incentives which encourage family breakdown, to the ultimate costs of society (in terms of increased welfare payments to single-parent families) and perhaps to couples themselves for whom the immediate attractions of divorce are very often followed by long-term unhappiness. Secondly, there is a widespread feeling that ordinary people, if not the 'liberal' elite, feel that human conduct is relevant to the divorce settlement, that some parties are treated unjustly by the law. This is illustrated dramatically in Australia where there have been physical attacks by outraged spouses on Family Court judges. In Britain, the campaign for justice in divorce has largely been led by aggrieved husbands compelled to pay maintenance to ex-wives (or face imprisonment) when they have done no wrong. Of course, wives often feel unjustly treated, especially when, as is often the case, particularly in America, their incomes fall relatively to those of their ex-husbands after divorce.

The restoration of the concept of marriage as a vow is clearly a non-starter. The hypocrisy and misery produced by very traditional marriage rules is quite inappropriate for the socially libertarian times in which we inescapably live. The vow aspect of marriage is now no more than decorative.

The only solution lies in some strengthening of the conventional features of marriage. This can be done in either a radical or a conservative way. The radical way would be to remove almost entirely (but not completely) the state from marriage and allow couples themselves to determine the form of marriage that they wish. They could decide in advance the terms of the contract and the procedures to be entered into if it should be breached. Couples could voluntarily decide, for example, what would happen in the event of either a mutually agreed or unilateral repudiation of the contract. They could, for example, restore adultery to its traditional role in the ancillaries. The state would be reduced to laying down universal obligations for the care of children and other (minor) ancillary conditions. Notice that this is quite different from pre-nuptial agreements that are often made in America. It is a feature of the common law that it is impossible for people to contract out of obligations imposed by a statute so that pre-nuptial agreements are necessarily limited in scope. If, for example, a marital 'offence', such as adultery is no longer, by statute, relevant to the divorce settlement then couples cannot by their own agreement make it so.

This radical version of contractualism has some attractions.[14] On the assumption that individuals are less permissive in their attitudes towards divorce than the state, it is quite likely that voluntary contracts would be more restrictive than the uniform one supplied by the monopoly state. Indeed, in Australia, the disgust felt by people towards the federal divorce law led to the growth of private contracts, often of a quite restrictive kind, which are enforced by the courts. What the parties to these agreements cannot do, though, is call themselves husband and wife.

The advantage of the extreme contractualist approach is that it draws attention to the need for 'pre-commitment', the idea that people would like some guarantee that their own behaviour, as well as that of others, will be restrained by a prior rule. It is a device to protect ourselves from the temptations of the *immediate*; temptations which may lead to long-term harm to ourselves. The fact that many people come to regret their divorces suggests that matters would improve if there were arrangements for pre-commitment. In economic examples, people may wish to supply voluntarily a public good, yet they need some assurance that individuals will not welsh on the deal. In the marital context, it is simply the recognition of the fact that individuals need some help in order to be moral. It is obvious that in the marriage law supplied by the state there is an extraordinarily inefficient form of pre-commitment.

Attractive though the radical contractarian model is I do not think that it is appropriate for marriage. The attempt to 'privatise' marriage in this way would be to deprive it of its significance as a social institution, whose public value is created by the approval of citizens, despite their departures from the moral standards that it sets. It is the one virtue of the vow theory of marriage that its stress on the public nature of the institution distinguishes it categorically from mere relationships, however well-protected by contract law. Individuals cannot, by their subjective choices, create marriage; it is a 'given', the value of which derives entirely from the fact it is not a voluntarily created institution (like a company).

This is perhaps why homosexual marriages should be excluded by the state. Their validation would damage what most people perceive to be a genuine public good. Of course, there is nothing in theory to stop homosexual couples making whatever private contracts they wish. Furthermore, since the state will inevitably be involved with important aspects of marriage, such as the care of children, the scope of individualism is necessarily limited.

Restructuring the State Marriage Contract

The restoration of pre-commitment will be better achieved by a rather more conservative solution: the restructuring of the state marriage contract. Only by this can personal liberty (which is denied by the vow theory) and justice be connected. This means that statute law should recognise that the marriage contract creates rights and obligations which must be justiciable: not merely because it is intrinsically right that they should be so but also because only these can provide the elements of pre-commitment which fragile and morally unreliable individuals so clearly need. Thus, while adultery, unreasonable behaviour and so on, need not be the sole grounds for divorce they should certainly feature strongly in the ancillaries. The law, for example, must provide that there should be a presumption (for obvious reasons) in favour of the mother having custody of children, but her claim could be countered, and modified, by clear evidence that her marital behaviour adversely affected her capacity here. However, the courts would make some allowance for a wife's contribution to home-making even if she were adjudged to be at fault.

People who enter marriage have a moral right to expect that marital duties will be performed reasonably and that adverse consequences will be visited on those who disregard them. Hence, if the state regards fidelity as a serious duty of marriage then it is just that spouses should 'pay' for any marital misdemeanour. If the distinguishing feature of marriage is that it is, or should be, a permanent arrangement, then obviously this creates expectations in both parties. To discount such expectations by refusing to admit obvious facts of wrong-doing into disputes over property and maintenance is to undermine the *meaning* of the marriage contract. The legal disputes that now take place on the dissolution of marriage may be fierce but they do not normally involve questions of conduct (although these may implicitly appear). Those who stress that conciliation should replace legalism have only half of the argument. Conciliation is, of course, desirable if reached mutually but not if it is 'imposed' by social workers or counsellors. This is, as the Australian experience shows, likely to lead to unpredictability.

Nothing in these proposed changes would prevent the unilateral repudiation of a marriage (it is not important in principle just how long a marriage should last before this is permissible). However, any spouse that so acts would forego any claim to (personal) maintenance, and the right to a share of the common property of the marriage would be qualified.

It has been suggested[15] that there should be an additional penalty against the wrongful party in a marital dispute: that he or she should be penalised for the withdrawal of that affection which is prescribed by the marriage contract. This seems to be highly contentious. People do not pre-commit themselves to undying love in a marital contract and the withdrawal of that surely cannot be compensated. They merely wish to protect themselves against more easily measurable adverse consequences of a marital break-up.

No doubt the objection to these tentative proposals to restore fully fault to the system of marital law will be that it is impossible to assign misconduct to particular parties, that (as judges and legislators in the 1960s and 1970s argued) marriages break down for a whole congeries of reasons which cannot be reduced to individual conduct. It is claimed that we cannot have the courts prying into the intimate secrets of a marriage. However, the objection derives from the dogma of the permissive era which maintained that nobody is to blame for anything. But as even the current British law grudgingly admits, but rarely applies, sometimes people are to blame: to argue that they are not is to imply that there ought to be freedom without responsibility in marital affairs. It is true that it might be difficult for the courts to assign fault, and that the attempt to do so will often reveal unpleasantness. But these are unfortunate facts of life: not insuperable barriers to the restoration of justice in marriage. In some cases, a breakdown would be mutually agreed so that no unpleasant court battles over fault would ensue.

It would, of course, be possible for couples to make subsidiary contracts within the broad statutory framework that restored the notion of fault. It is here that pre-nuptial contracts would come into play. They would obviously relate to matters concerning the property that is brought into a marriage by one or both parties. The title to this therefore would not be affected by conduct in the marriage.

The Child Support Agency

The current controversy over the working of the Child Support Agency has renewed interest in the concept of justice in marriage. The Agency, which came into operation in 1993, has the laudable aim of tracking down absent fathers and enforcing on them maintenance orders. The main complaint has been that it is more concerned with efficiency than with justice. It has increased the maintenance orders of ex-husbands (who may very well have remarried) rather than pursued non-payers.

A further objection is that the Agency apparently has the authority to over-rule 'clean break' agreements originally negotiated between divorcing spouses. Some husbands have argued that they signed away valuable property rights, usually the equity in the marital home, in order to be freed of future maintenance obligations. It is, of course, true that the law did not permit a 'clean break' with children, but injustices are clearly occurring. Is there not a problem of 'moral hazard' here, i.e. the creation of an incentive for an ex-wife to go to the Child Support Agency to secure maintenance *after* a 'clean break'? The aim of the Agency is clearly to reduce the costs of income support and not the achievement of justice in marriage and divorce.

It is too early to assess all the effects of the new arrangements but it is certain that post-marital bitterness will be intensified. Already there is a demand from aggrieved ex-husbands that original 'clean break' settlements should be renegotiated in the context of new maintenance orders imposed by the Child Support Agency. It is well worth suggesting that the current injustices could have been avoided if fault had been a factor in the original divorce settlements. That would not have removed the obligations of an ex-husband to his children but it would certainly have affected the nature of the 'clean break'.

Justice and 'Social' Justice in Marriage

Feminist critics of my proposals fully to restore fault to the system of marital law might argue that they are subtly designed to favour men over women in marital disputes. Most divorces are initiated by women and in Britain the favoured ground for a 'quickie' divorce is unreasonable behaviour, which is hardly worth defending in the current legal context. It is easy to demonstrate. Today, even if men successfully launch a divorce petition against

their wives for adultery (the most popular male ground) or
unreasonable behaviour they, since husbands are normally the
major income earners, will still have to bear the costs of
maintenance and will lose property. Am I not recommending a
solution which will restore a *status quo ante* which it is said
always favoured men over women? Will it simply encourage a
rush of petitions by husbands?

This charge has to be taken seriously. It is supported by the
facts that, in America especially, women are worse off financially
than men after divorce.[16] Maintenance orders are difficult to
enforce (alimony payments tend to be temporary in America so
that once the value and division of such things as the house and
other assets are settled the husband is more or less free of
obligations) and, since women normally have custody of the
children, they are less able to participate in the re-marriage
market.

Susan Okin[17] has argued that the absence of justice in
American marriage means that the law treats women as equals
when the conditions of marriage renders them unequal. A crucial
point in her argument is that the most important source of
family wealth is human capital (normally the husband's future
earning power). Since divorced women have a much diluted claim
over this in divorce settlements they are (for this and other
reasons) unjustly treated by the law. She rightly points out the
adverse effects that no fault divorce laws have on women,
although she does not see the importance of this in the context
of a theory of formal justice.

However, we should treat the fact of a divorced wife's reduced
income with a little caution. A person's welfare is by no means
solely a function of his or her income. For example, if a wife
voluntarily repudiates a marriage then even though she may
forego some or all of her husband's future income, she is still
better off. She is freed from a presumably irksome husband. Her
lowered income is simply a cost she has to bear in order to
increase her overall welfare (of which not being married is a
part). Under my proposals, if a husband repudiates the marriage
he would not be relieved of maintenance costs (which would be
rigorously enforced, possibly for a life-time) and his share of
property would be proportionate to his fault. Indeed, the
existence of fault provisions in the law would put wives in a
much stronger bargaining position. The fact that women normally

secure custody of children, and hence are likely to have a low standard of living, should not itself justify an automatic redistribution of income from husbands to wives. Some men want custody, even though they normally lose custody battles, and it would be unjust in such cases to insist that husbands should make *extra* payments to ex-wives, except where the man is at fault. The welfare of wives is increased by having custody of children despite their cost. Many men certainly regard themselves in these cases as worse off for not securing custody. Justice would only be achievable in such obviously difficult matters if consideration of conduct were relevant to the proceedings.

It seems to me that Professor Okin does not appreciate the full significance of the fault provision as a *procedural* device for securing justice in marriage. Her claim is that in principle 'both post-divorce households should enjoy the same standard of living'.[18] This, however, is an egalitarian claim that for her should characterise all post-marital relationships, irrespective of conduct. It is justified, apparently on the ground that men's income is normally higher anyway. But can it be just that a husband should be obliged to pay for an erring wife indefinitely? Does a divorced wife have a claim on (possibly unexpected) increases in an ex-husband's income irrespective of the circumstances of the breakdown? It seems to be quite wrong to use the marriage laws as some kind of device to correct the inequalities of income between men and women that may emerge spontaneously from market processes. Professor Okin wishes to create 'social' justice in marriage (and post-marriage) rather than justice.

My agenda would not correct these inequalities but it would certainly reduce the well-being of some men that obtains under the present law. Philandering, and drunken or violent, husbands would have to pay the costs of their behaviour. The rigorous enforcement of maintenance orders would relieve the state of some of the costs of one-parent families. Equally important is the fact that the change in the incentive structure that the reintroduction of fault would entail provides that pre-commitment which is essential if the stability of the family is to be restored. Proposals such as this represent an important repudiation of some of the worst features of the permissive society. This seems to be a more feasible aim than the attempt to introduce a highly contentious egalitarianism into an already complex area.

Notes

1 See Davies, J., (ed.), Berger, B. and Carlson, A., *The Family: Is It Just Another Lifestyle Choice?*, London: IEA Health and Welfare Unit, 1993.

2 *Marriage and Divorce Statistics 1991: England and Wales*, Series FM2 no. 19, HMSO, 1993.

3 Hegel, G.W.F., *The Philosophy of Right*, Translated by W. Knox, Oxford: Clarendon Press, 1952, ch. 4.

4 *Ibid.*, p. 113.

5 See Davis, G. and Murch, M., *Grounds for Divorce*, Oxford: Clarendon Press, 1988, ch. 4.

6 Mount, F., *The Subversive Family*, London: Unwin, 1982.

7 Milton's *The Doctrine and Discipline of Divorce* is discussed in Mount, *op. cit.*, pp. 209-13.

8 For details of British law see Davis and Murch, *op. cit.*; and Glendon, M.A., *The Transformation of Family Law*, Chicago: University of Chicago Press, 1989, ch. 4.

9 See Davis and Murch, *op. cit.*, pp. 14-17.

10 Quoted in Davis and Murch, *op. cit.*, p. 16.

11 Matrimonial and Family Proceedings Act (1984).

12 See Morgan, P., 'Fidelity in the Family: Once Absolute, Now Another "Choice"', in Anderson D., (ed.), *The Loss of Virtue*, London: The Social Affairs Unit, 1993, pp. 99-118.

13 See Becker, *op. cit.*, ch. 10.

14 I took this view once myself, see Barry, N., 'An Individualist's View of Marriage and the Family', *Policy Report*, 1989, pp. 37-39.

15 This seems to be the implication of the argument of Maley, B., *Marriage, Divorce and Family Justice*, Sydney: Centre for Independent Studies, 1993, pp. 38-40, where he suggests that damages should be paid to a wronged party in addition to the claim that the ancillaries should be decided on grounds of fault. This book is, incidentally, a good introduction to the subject and contains useful Australian material.

16 'Separate but Unequal: The Economic Disaster for Women and Children', *Family Law Quarterly*, 1987.

17 Okin, S., *Justice, Gender and the Family*, New York: Basic Books, 1989.

18 *Ibid.*, p. 183.

Taking Stock: Assessing Twenty Years of 'No fault' Divorce

Bryce J Christensen

J UST over twenty years ago, California lawmakers initiated a revolution in family law by abolishing the traditional requirement that divorce be granted only after establishing fault for the violation of the wedding vow. California's new 'no fault' law further permitted one spouse to unilaterally abrogate the wedding vow. Some commentators have hailed California's new 'no fault' statute as 'a milestone in the modernisation of laws relating to marriage and divorce' and as 'a landmark event in American legal history.'[1] Supporters of the new law expressed hopes that it would 'reduce the acrimony, hostility, and bitterness in the divorce process.'[2] The very year that California's 'no fault' law went into effect one legal scholar praised the California State Bar as 'perhaps the most far-sighted of such institutions in America' for advocating the new law, while he lauded the supportive state legislators 'for the courage in instituting a most necessary though highly controversial element of social reform.' 'No fault' divorce, this scholar declared, had not only 'erased the anachronisms from California divorce law', but had also 'removed once and for all from the divorce action the tragic-comedy of the adversary proceeding. It can be expected that the California reform will chart the path for the civilisation of domestic relations law throughout the United States,' he predicted.[3]

California's 'no fault' divorce law rapidly did become a model for other states. Endorsed in 1970 by the National Conference of Commissioners on Uniform State Laws (NCCUSL), 'no fault' divorce rapidly won acceptance nationwide. Between 1970 and 1975, state lawmakers enacted 'a landslide of liberalising

This chapter first appeared as an article in *The Family in America* (September 1991), the magazine of The Rockford Institute Center on the Family in America. Reproduced by kind permission.

legislation.' By 1976, legislators in 11 states had followed California in establishing 'irretrievable' marriage breakdown as the sole ground of divorce, while 36 other states had less dramatically abandoned traditional divorce law based exclusively on fault. Three-fourths of these states also followed California in permitting unilateral divorce. In 1985, South Dakota became the last state in the Union to adopt a version of 'no fault' divorce.[4]

In their crusade for 'no fault' divorce, advocates have achieved stunning success against remarkably little resistance. Despite its radical break with tradition, the legal rationale of 'no fault' divorce has seldom received sceptical scrutiny. And even twenty years after enactment, few have examined the social consequences of adopting 'no fault' divorce. A hard look at a soft law is long overdue.

Revolution From the Top

Sober analysis of 'no fault' divorce may properly begin with a recognition that when legislators made this revolutionary break with legal tradition, they were not responding to widespread public pressure, but rather acceding to the well-orchestrated lobbying of a few activists. Legal scholar Herbert Jacob points out that the ideas marshalled to justify 'no fault' divorce 'remained confined to a narrow élite of attorneys and therapists and were not widely diffused in the general legal literature on divorce before the 1970s.' The enactment of 'no fault' divorce proceeded 'with little publicity and no mass support.' Eclipsed in the media and in public forums by other issues—such as civil rights, Vietnam, Watergate, and abortion—divorce reform never emerged as a major issue for political debate. 'The general public,' Jacob remarks, 'was never mobilised to concern itself with divorce law changes during election campaigns, when the general public is most likely to be attentive to policy issues.' As a consequence, 'those who had experienced divorce and those who might resort to it in the future did not help define the issues.' At both the state and national level, 'no fault' divorce proceeded to passage largely in 'obscurity and under ... control of experts'. Consequently, 'no fault' divorce came into law by passing through the democratic forms of state legislatures, but without ever acquiring much democratic substance. In following the recommending of NCCUSL, many legislators voted for 'no fault' statutes supposing the proposed changes were simply 'technical' legal adjustments. In this dubious fashion, a radical legal concept espoused by a few specialists became a law which has profoundly affected the lives of millions.[5]

Though never widely demanded by the general public, 'no fault' divorce did garner support from many divorce lawyers weary of the deceit and hypocrisy common in adversarial divorce proceedings. In traditional divorce proceedings, courtroom investigations into infidelity were often stage-acted using a 'script' prearranged by the estranged spouses. In other cases, embittered spouses would engage private investigators to gather evidence through unethical violations of privacy. 'No fault' divorce appeared to offer an easier and less contentious way to end a marriage. No one denies the abuses under the old law nor the advantages in the new law for divorce lawyers and some clients. But when the question is one of abrogating vows, the search for a clean, convenient path may do violence to legal reasoning and the demands of justice.

Clear thinking about divorce must begin with clear thinking about marriage. A husband and wife marry through solemn vows, pronounced before witnesses. Generally, these vows include the words 'until death do us part,' or some similar phrase. Though most weddings in the United States have since colonial times been solemnised by religious authorities, traditional legal theory acknowledged the state's interest in protecting wedding vows. Articulating this theory in 1888, the U.S. Supreme Court declared that 'other contracts may be modified, restricted or enlarged, or entirely released upon the consent of the parties. Not so with marriage. The relation once formed, the law steps in and holds the parties to various obligations and liabilities. It is an institution, the purity of which the public is deeply interested in, for it is the foundation of the family and society without which there would be neither civilization nor progress'. Further, the High Court reasoned, the obligations of marriage 'arise not from the consent of concurring minds, but are the creation of the law itself: a relation the most important, as affecting the happiness of individuals, the first step from barbarism to incipient civilization, the purest tie of social life and the true basis of human progress'.[6]

In its full rigour, the traditional view enunciated by the High Court made it almost impossible to obtain a divorce. Represent-

ative of traditional opposition to divorce, Timothy Dwight, an
early president of Yale, argued that 'it is incomparably better
that individuals should suffer than that an institution (i.e.
marriage), which is the basis of all human good, should be
shaken, or endangered'.[7] Nonetheless, nineteenth-century laws
typically allowed for divorce on grounds of adultery or desertion.
State legislatures also granted divorces on other grounds on a
case-by-case basis during the nineteenth century. When the
burden of deciding legislative divorces became too great, many
state legislatures authorized the courts to add such failings as
alcoholism, insanity, and cruelty to the list of legal warrants for
divorce. In a few states—most notoriously Nevada—the statutes
governing divorce became especially lax in this century. Nonetheless, until California enacted 'no fault' divorce, the traditional
view prevailed that the state had a vital interest in protecting
the marriage vows which it authorized by issuing a wedding
license and that this vital interest required some finding of
culpability when those vows were broken. 'No fault' divorce put
the state—for the first time—in the absurd position of requiring
a license for the pronouncing of public vows which the state
subsequently regards with indifference. Warning against just
such an absurdity, Congressman Robert F. Drinan wrote in 1968
that 'if American divorce law in the near future formally
endorses the idea that spouses may rescind their contract of
marriage by mutual choice and without any allegation or proof
of fault, American law may well have explicitly or implicitly
rejected the concept of marriage as a status or as an
institution'.[8] In explaining 'no fault' divorce as part of a 'dejurid-
ification of marriage', noted legal scholar Mary Ann Glendon
cites the argument that 'a relationship which can be freely
entered or left is not a legal relationship; whatever else it may
be'.[9] Lloyd Cohen compares marriage under a regime of 'no fault'
divorce to 'the contract at will in the ordinary employment
context', but admits that 'it is hardly so durable' in its legal
force.[10] The question, then, that advocates of 'no fault' divorce
have never answered is simple, but disturbing: why does the
state continue to issue wedding licenses for the saying of vows
now robbed of legal meaning and reduced to less than the
weakest of contracts?

'No Fault' divorce trivializes both marriage and the powers of
the court. In 1977 Mary Ann Glendon wrote that although 'the

form of judicial inquest was preserved' under no fault, 'it is clear that under the California and other no-fault laws the "inquest" is nothing more than a ritual; and that divorce is, in fact if not in form, available upon unilateral demand'. Glendon goes so far as to say that, aside from financial disputes, 'modern divorce proceedings often do not resemble a regular lawsuit so much as what would appear to an anthropologist to be a ritual change of status'.[11] But how is it possible that American jurists now consent to enact legally vapid rituals upon demand? For those who regard the separation of church and state as essential to America's constitutional order, it can hardly be a trivial concern that the judiciary now ritually invalidates vows pronounced sacred by religious authority—without any governing legal rationale to guide these ritual invalidations. In our current culture of permissive sex and cohabitation, many marriages would break up even under traditional laws. But the state need not set itself up in the business of ceremonially legitimating such ruptures. If the state refuses to consider fault, what can it do when granting divorces but enact a secular rite of absolution, so authorising the former spouses to be respectably relicensed to again say marriage vows—which can yet again be violated without legal acknowledgment or culpable behaviour?

Subverting Marriage

By adopting 'no fault' divorce statues, the state adopts a posture which is actually more subversive of marriage than mere indifference. For by making it easy to void a wedding vow without incurring legal guilt, the state discourages self-sacrifice and emotional commitment to the marriage. Author Lenore Weitzman believes that 'a radical change in the rules for ending marriage inevitably affects the rules for marriage itself and the intentions and expectations of those who enter it'. 'No fault' divorce, she reasons, is now 'redefining marriage as a time-limited, contingent arrangement rather than a lifelong commitment'.[12] Partly because of 'the failure of the legal system' to protect spouses against divorce, Cohen sees many Americans choosing to 'invest less in this marriage or in being married'. In particular, he suspects that many women may be 'investing fewer resources in being wives in general and in being one man's wife in particular in fear of uncompensated breach'.[13]

Attorney Arlynn Leiber Presser likewise sees 'the problem of divorce and its tendency to create strategic behavior within the family unit'. 'If the assumption is that a marriage will end in divorce', Presser asks, 'why should my party take any selfless action? And, in fact, why should the party with the most to lose from divorce ever contemplate entering this formerly holy and eternal union at all?'[14]

Not surprisingly, fear of divorce is one of the primary reasons that an increasing number of young adults cohabit outside marriage. But cohabitation generally fails as a strategy for protecting against divorce: most couples who cohabit do eventually marry, but their marriages prove much *more* fragile than those of couples who do not cohabit before marriage.[15] The shadow of 'no fault' divorce has also fallen on many men and women who married before 1970, little suspecting that the state would retroactively undermine the legal force and meaning of their vows. Because divorce rates were surging upwards *before* the enactment of 'no fault' laws, many investigators have concluded that such legislation had little or no effect upon the incidence of divorce. However, in two recent studies—one at the University of Chicago and one at Justec Research in Virginia—researchers have established that 'no fault' statutes did significantly drive up the divorce rate in a number of states. In his 1989 Justec investigation of the effects of 'no fault' divorce in 38 states, lawyer and sociologist Thomas B. Marvell uncovered 'very strong evidence' that adoption of 'no fault' had led to more divorces in eight states (including California) and found 'some lesser evidence of the laws' impacts in eight more' (including New York). As a 'rough estimate' of the effects of 'no fault' laws in these 16 states (including the two most populous in the country), Marvell concludes that 'on average, the no fault laws increased divorces by some 20 to 25 per cent'. In other words, adoption of 'no fault' divorce has led to tens of thousands of divorces that would not have occurred under traditional law. On the other hand, Marvell could find 'no evidence of reverse causation: that is, divorce rate growth leading to new laws'.[16] Even in the states in which 'no fault' statutes have no statistically demonstrable effect on rising divorce rates, the adoption of such statutes may be regarded as a highly questionable legal accommodation to an unfavourable social trend. When any behaviour—drug use, prostitution, dumping of toxic waste, divorce—becomes more common, state authorities take the easy, but not necessarily the best, way out by simply abolishing or weakening the legal restrictions against such behaviour.

Defenders of 'no fault' statutes often argue that, as a deeply personal decision, divorce ought to by left to individuals, without state interference. This argument dissolves under examination. Divorce is not simply a personal decision, for it imposes tremendous costs on people who have not made that choice. First, and most obviously, divorce brings heavy, often tragic emotional and personal burdens to spouses who do not want to dissolve their marriages. Even under fault-based laws, many men and women suffered the heartbreak of divorces they did not want. But 'no fault' divorce, especially when it permits unilateral divorce, implicitly allies the state with spouses who want *out* of their marriages. 'A major consequence of the no-consent standard', Weitzman observes, 'has been to shift the power from the spouse who wants to remain married to the spouse who wants to get divorced'. Accordingly, 'the new law elevates one's "right" to divorce over a spouse's "right" to remain married'.[17]

Weitzman reports that many men and women have been shocked and surprised to learn that their spouses could dissolve their marriages without establishing culpability and even without mutual consent. While it has undermined the status of both husbands and wives, 'no fault' divorce has especially exposed traditional homemakers to betrayal and abandonment. While almost two-thirds of petitions for divorce are still filed by women, the fraction of such petitions filed by men rose sharply upon passage of 'no fault' divorce.[18] In the era of 'no fault' many men have forgotten what little they previously knew about chivalry and self-restraint.

Into Poverty

For many women, 'no fault' divorce has meant impoverishment as well as heartache. Following enactment of 'no fault' divorce, judges ceased to order the payment of alimony except for short periods, since a finding of spousal guilt had previously provided the rationale for most such awards. Indeed, under 'no fault', wives are 'increasingly required to assist in the liquidation of predivorce debt'. For a similar reason, the percentage of cases in which wives receive more than half of the household assets has also dropped sharply. Whereas a former wife usually received the family home under traditional law, 'equitable division' under 'no fault' typically means a forced sale of the home to divide the equity.[19] Even defenders of the 'no fault' such as Riane Tennenhaus Eisler concede that 'the elimination of guilt and innocence has also taken away from divorce proceedings some of the weapons lawyers traditionally used to get better economic settlements for wives'.[20] Because 'no fault' divorce has weakened (though hardly overthrown) the legal presumption favouring maternal custody in divorce proceedings, many women have surrendered many of their economic claims in order to prevent a custody fight.

Using some questionable statistical methods, Weitzman has asserted that under 'no fault' divorce, 'divorced women and the minor children in their households experience a 73 per cent decline in their standard of living in the first year after divorce'.[21] More plausible, but still deeply sobering, is Kate J., Stirling's 1989 finding that among divorced women who do not remarry, 'in the initial years of divorce, economic well-being declines by more than 30 per cent and remains at that same low level' for many years.[22] Terry Arendell reports that middle-class women often have no idea of 'the kind of hardship they will face after divorce'. Divorce pushes many into poverty or near poverty.[23]

On the other hand, 'no fault' divorce has also encouraged opportunistic behaviour by faithless wives. Even when the wife has first betrayed her husband and then initiated the divorce, 'no fault' divorce frequently gives her one-half of the household assets *and* custody of the children. Justice Richard Neely of the West Virginia Supreme Court acknowledges that 'a blameless father often emerges from divorce courts with all the financial responsibility of marriage and none of its emotional or economic rewards'. Not infrequently, an innocent father is 'saddled with children whom he never sees and who may even have been turned against him'.[24]

Weitzman has claimed that in the first year after a divorce, men on average 'experience a 42 per cent rise in their standard of living'.[25] But this statistic is as suspect as her figure for the economic status of women after divorce. Criticizing Weitzman's numbers, Jed Abraham observes that 'men in particular experience losses ... that are not easily quantifiable'. He points out that many divorced men 'will have left single-family homes for small apartments. They will have exchanged home-cooked meals for fast-food fare'. In general, Abraham finds that among divorced men 'their standard of *family* living declines precipitously' after a 'no fault' divorce.[26]

The ambiguities of individual cases defy global pronouncements about the relative effects of 'no fault' divorce on men and women. However, what *is* beyond doubt is that contemporary divorce is rarely a benefit to *both* the former husband *and* the former wife. In a 10-year study of middle-class California couples divorced in 1970 and 1971 (the first years of 'no fault'), Judith Wallerstein found that 'in most families the divorce had eventuated in an enhanced quality of life for only one of the divorce partners ... Their former spouses either experienced significantly diminished quality of life or were living in conditions that, on balance, were equivalent to the stresses and gratifications during the failed marriage'. In one-fifth of the divorces Wallerstein investigated, '*both* of the former marital partners were living in significantly worsened situations' than they had been while in their troubled marriages. 'The quality of life had demonstrably improved for *both* of the former partners after only one-tenth of the divorces Wallerstein examined. Wallerstein reported that 'anger rooted in the sense of having been exploited and rejected remained high in 40 percent of the women and in close to 30 percent of the men' ten years after their divorces.[27] Such findings cast doubt on the claims that 'no fault' provisions take the acrimony out of divorce. Anger and a sense of injustice may even be intensified by the perception that the state passively acquiesces in a spouse's infidelity. Nor have easier divorce laws changed a persistent pattern: divorced men and women suffer from poorer physical and mental health than married men and women.[28] A number of studies have also established a correlation between divorce and suicide,[29] giving forceful confirmation of G.K. Chesterton's remark that we should 'regard a system that produces many divorces as we do a system that drives men to drown or shoot themselves'.[30]

Easy legal divorce consequently proves a dubious and partial benefit even for many who suppose they want it. Divorce, as Cohen points out, may be 'the legal dissolution of marriage, but it does not by itself unscramble the complex arrangement that preceded it'.[31] Social worker June Gary Hopps complains that 'there is too little recognition that the quick and easy cessation of a legal marriage contract fosters an illusion that the dissolution of a relationship is just as easy and unencumbered'.[32] In a survey of divorced parents conducted by the University of Virginia in 1976, researchers discovered that two years after the event, about two-thirds of 'former marriage partners thought the divorce might have been a mistake and that they should have tried harder to resolve their conflicts'.[33]

Innocent Victims

While it may be difficult to allocate blame for the failure of marriages, that blame virtually never belongs on those who often feel guilty nonetheless—that is the children. Psychologists report that an irrational sense of guilt is common among children of divorce.[34] 'No fault' divorces have not dispelled that sense of guilt, nor have they even contradicted it by assigning culpability to either or both of the parents. Meanwhile, the number of children living with the aftermath of parental divorce has risen since 'no fault' became the law, despite a marked fall in overall fertility. While only 13 children per 1,000 children were involved in a parental divorce in 1970 when 'no fault' began, that figure had risen to 19 per 1,000 by 1981 and stood at 17 per 1,000 in 1986. The annual number of children involved in parental divorce stood at 870,000 in 1970, rose to almost 1,200,000 and settled to just over 1,000,000 in 1986.[35]

Almost all (88 per cent) of children in single-parent households live with their mothers rather than their fathers.[36] Inevitably, children share in the privations of divorced mothers. Over half (56 per cent) of children in female-headed households live in poverty, compared to just one-eighth (13 per cent) of children in two-parent and male-headed households.[37] The children often suffer from deprivations not merely monetary. Many suffer from a paternal deprivation caused either by their fathers' lack of interest or by their mothers' hostility toward their former spouses. Among children of divorced parents who live with their mothers, less than half will see their fathers at all during a given year.[38] One national survey found that among children not living with a divorced father, only ten per cent maintained 'regular contact' over a five year period and only five per cent maintained regular contact over ten years. The loss of father-child contacts appears especially notable 'among children whose fathers moved out when they were quite young—many of whom lose contact with their fathers for most or all of their childhood'.[39]

Sociologist Alan Booth fears that 'the weakened child-father bond will perpetuate itself into future generations' so that 'the family system becomes one dominated by the mother-child bond, with males playing only an incidental role in the social lives of children', resulting in 'shallow male-female relationships and a social system that rests on the worst features of male dominance and aggression and female nurturance'.[40]

Beyond the deprivations of poverty, children living without their fathers are more vulnerable to a number of social and personal ills less often found among children living with both parents. Compared to children living with both parents, children living in single-parent households are more likely to fail in school, to suffer poorer physical and mental health, to suffer abuse or neglect, to commit crimes or to be victims of crime, to bear or beget children out of wedlock, to use alcohol or drugs, and to be unemployed as young adults.[41] Even suicide among teens and young adults appears traceable to parental divorce.[42] Sociologist Sara McLanahan finds that remarriage by divorced mothers apparently does not remove many of the problems found among the children of single-parent households. 'In statistical profile, children living in stepfamilies look much like children of unmarried parents in their propensity to drop out of school, bear an illegitimate child, or to be unemployed during young adult-hood'.[43] 'We have made a mistake', declares Justice Neely, 'by not paying greater attention to how our new divorce-on-demand system is affecting a generation of children brought up in the poverty of single-parent homes'.[44]

Justice Neely further observes that 'when lack of family stability causes failure in school, delinquency, or drug dependency, it is not the family involved who must foot the bill to redeem their troubled children. All the rest of society—through such government social service programs as drug treatment centers, special schools, residential halfway houses, social workers, and probation officers—ends up paying'.[45] Informed taxpayers might especially resent carrying such social burdens at a time when state officials do nothing to prevent the casual divorces which help create such burdens. Taxpayers who have preserved their own marriages through personal integrity and sacrifice may find it puzzling and offensive that state officials appear so willing to dissolve marriages and to collectivize the costs.

To properly assess the injustice for taxpayers of 'no fault' divorce, other government policies which undermine marriage need to be considered. Researchers have repeatedly established that contemporary welfare programmes, especially Aid to Families with Dependent Children (AFDC), foster both divorce and illegitimacy.[46] The adoption of 'no fault' statutes reinforces such effects, further transforming government into an institution virulently subversive of marriage.

Meagre Gains

More than twenty years after enactment of 'no fault' divorce, can proponents point to no favourable outcomes of the new law? Legal scholars have noted 'a dramatic decline in the number of litigious actions preceding the interlocutory decree' of divorce after 'no fault' statutes were enacted, a pattern suggesting that 'some of the acrimony and hostility engendered by the former adversary system has been diluted, as reformers intended'.[47] But not everyone has been convinced that 'no fault' statutes have reduced acrimony in divorce. 'Has hostility been decreased [by "no fault" laws]?' asked Elizabeth Guhring in 1981 as a past president of the Women's Bar Association of the District of Columbia. 'Is the divorce process less traumatic? I do not know, and in the absence of qualitative or quantitative studies, it is difficult to tell'.[48] The proposition that 'no fault' laws dissipate acrimony finds no support in Wallerstein's discovery of relatively high prevalence of unresolved rage among men and women who had gone through 'no fault' divorces ten years earlier. Even as a strategy for reducing litigation, 'no fault' divorce may succeed only in the short run. Attorney Steven K. Ward reports that because of 'the trend of trial courts toward equal property division' under 'no fault' divorce laws, 'the stage is set for an increase in tort claims and counterclaims in divorce litigation'.[49] Apparently, the 'fault' which reformers thought they had thrown out the back door is now banging on the front door as a tort.

Easy divorce has not even reduced the likelihood that couples will stay together in an unhappy marriage. According to national surveys taken from the early 1970s to the late 1980s, the probability that men and women will report being 'in a poor marriage has *increased* slightly'. At the same time, a decreasing proportion of couples report 'marital happiness', apparently because of a reluctance by men and women to 'commit fully' to a union they expect may not last.[50] The shadow of causal divorce has thus chilled many homes in which couples do not separate.

In any case, the courts' refusal to consider fault in divorce cases is hardly a part of a general contraction of the courts' functions. On the contrary, historians see the state taking on new powers, as 'courts have permitted government intrusion into areas traditionally regarded as bastions of family autonomy'.[51] For instance, the courts have increased their powers to investigate and prosecute marital rape and domestic violence. Further, at the very time that the courts have shirked their traditional responsibility to consider fault in terminating marriages, they have expanded their regulatory powers over employers terminating contracts of employees.[52] 'No fault' divorce does not reflect a new libertarian or *laissez-faire* attitude governing the courts in general. Rather, the suspicion grows that G.K. Chesterton was right when he identified 'the trend toward divorce' as part of 'that modern change which would make the state infinitely superior to the Family'.[53] Mary Ann Glendon seems close to admitting as much when she observes that contemporary Americans are 'loosely held in their families, closely bound to occupational or government-derived statutes'. In this social order, she acknowledges, rules of law serve not to bind individual to individual (as in marriage), but rather to assign individuals to their 'niches in the social structure'.[54] For those who recognize with Swan the traditional importance of the family as 'a freestanding institution mediating between the individual citizen and the central government', the easy dissolution of marital and family ties can only make it harder for Americans to 'organize their lives independently of central political authority'.[55]

Legal integrity, social health, and political liberty all require of the nation's lawmakers a critical reassessment of 'no fault' divorce. Though now well entrenched in every state, 'no fault' has recently aroused opposition that may signal a promising shift. For instance, in the spring of 1991, legislators in Washington introduced three different bills to reintroduce fault into divorce proceedings. The first bill would have fully restored the

fault system in effect until 1973 in Washington. A second bill
would have permitted 'no fault' divorce, but allowed judges to
consider marital misconduct in making property settlements. The
third bill would have permitted couples to make premarital
agreements requiring a finding of fault should their marriage
fail.[56] None of the bills passed, yet sponsors (who were encouraged by more support than anticipated) plan to reintroduce this
legislation again. In introducing the statute allowing couples to
enter binding premarital agreements, the Washington legislators
were actually drawing upon a model statute promulgated by the
American Legislative Exchange Council (ALEC). A version of this
same model statute has recently been introduced in Illinois,
where it passed the senate, though it stalled in the house of
representatives.[57] Other state legislatures will likely consider
similar measures in the near future. But while some state
legislators consider undoing 'no fault' divorce law, an important
test case in Pennsylvania may force the judiciary to consider its
constitutionality. In the case *Witcher v. Witcher*, Phyllis Witcher
is arguing that 'not to consider who is the breaching party of a
marital contract is unconstitutional, because it denies the party
who wishes to uphold the contract the right to due process in
the protection of his or her property'. No plaintiff has ever
litigated this issue before, so observers believe this may prove a
very important case.[58] Mounting a more problematic challenge to
'no fault', some feminists are now advocating that the basic
premises of 'no fault' continue to govern divorce, but that judges
follow new formulas to ensure that women—especially mothers—receive more generous settlements. Weitzman belongs to this
camp, insisting that despite its 'unanticipated, unintended, and
unfortunate consequences', 'no fault' divorce is still 'a major step
forward' in law, needing only some adjustments to 'provide
economic protection for women and children'.[59] Because of such
ideological schizophrenia, few feminists share the wisdom of
Arlynn Lieber Presser who in the pages of the *American Bar
Association Journal* recently hoped for 'the day when a truly
radical feminist proposes marriage for life, only dissolvable under
extreme circumstances'.[60] Rather, most feminist activists are
rallying around proposals on child support and property division
that would discourage men from entering marriage while
reducing the incentives for women to work out the difficulties in
a strained union.[61]

Few observers would venture to predict just what course legislators and judges will follow as they consider divorce law in the years ahead. But it is past time to repudiate the hysterical rhetoric of those who once regarded 'no fault' divorce as a milestone in the advancement of American civilization. If it is a milestone at all, it marks movement on a legal and cultural path that tends downward.

Notes

1   Dixon, R.B. and Weitzman, L.J., 'Evaluating the Impact of No-Fault Divorce in California', *Family Relations* 29, 1980, p. 297; Eisler, R.T., *Dissolution: No-Fault Divorce, Marriage, and the Future of Women,* New York: McGraw-Hill, 1977, p. 5.

2   Weitzman L.J., *The Divorce Revolution: The Unexpected Social and Economic Consequences for Women and Children in America*, New York: The Free Press, 1985, p. ix.

3   Krom H.A., 'California's Divorce Law Reform: An Historical Analysis', *Pacific Law Journal*, 1 1970, p. 181.

4   Marvell, T.B., 'Divorce Rates and the Fault Requirement', *Law and Society Review*, 23, 1989, p. 544; Glendon, M.A., *State, Law, and Family: Family Law in Transition in the United States and Western Europe,* Oxford: North-Holland, 1977, p. 227; Freed, D.J. and Foster, H.H., 'Family Law in the Fifty States: An Overview', *Family Law Quarterly,* 17 1984, p. 373; Kay, H.H., 'Beyond No-Fault: New Directions in Divorce Reform', in Sugarman, S.D. and Kay, H.H. (eds.), *Divorce Reform at the Crossroads*, New Haven: State University Press, 1990, p. 6.

5   Jacob H., *Silent Revolution: The Transformation of Divorce Law in the United States,* Chicago: University of Chicago Press, 1988, pp. 65-69, 150-51.

6   *Maynard v. Hill*, 125 U.S. 190, 1888, cited in Howell, J.C., *No-Fault Divorce: The Citizen's Legal Guide,* Englewood Cliffs: Prentice-Hall, 1981, pp. 6-7.

7   Dwight cited in Blake, N.M., *The Road to Reno: A History of Divorce in the United States*, New York: Macmillan, 1962, p. 58.

8   Drinan cited in Glendon, M.A., *op. cit.,* p. 236.

9   Glendon, M.A., *op. cit.*, p. 236.

10 Cohen, L., 'Marriage, Divorce, and Quasi Rents; Or, "I Gave Him the Best Years of My Life"', *Journal of Legal Studies*, 16, 1987, p. 299.

11 Glendon, M.A., *The Transformation of Family Law: State, Law, and Family in the United States and Western Europe*, Chicago: University of Chicago Press, 1989, p. 195.

12 Weitzman, L., 'The Divorce Law Revolution and the Transformation of Legal Marriage', in Davis, K. (ed.), *Contemporary Marriage: Comparative Perspectives on a Changing Institution*, New York: Russell Sage, 1985, pp. 305, 335.

13 Cohen, L., *op. cit.*, p. 295.

14 Presser, A.L., 'Divorce American Style', rev. of Kay, H.H. and Sugarman, S.D. (eds.), *Divorce Reform at the Crossroads*, *ABA Journal*, April 1991, pp. 124-25.

15 See Bumpass, L.L. and Sweet, J.A., 'National Estimates of Cohabitation: Cohort Levels and Union Stability', NSFH Working Paper No. 2, Center for Demography and Ecology, University of Wisconsin, June 1989.

16 Marvell, T.B., *op. cit.* pp. 559-63.

17 Weitzman, L.J., *op. cit.*, p. 27.

18 US Department of Health and Human Services, 'Advance Report of Final Divorce Statistics, 1988', *Monthly Vital Statistics Report*, Vol. 39, No. 12, Supplement 2, 1991, p. 5; Dixon, R.B. and Weitzman, L.J., 'When Husbands File for Divorce', *Journal of Marriage and the Family*, 44, 1982, pp. 103-114.

19 Weitzman, L.J., *op. cit.*, pp. 78-79, p. 369; Dixon, R.B. and Weitzman, L.J., *op. cit.*, pp. 305-36; Welch III, C.E. and Price-Bonham, S., 'A Decade of No-Fault Divorce Revisited: California, Georgia, and Washington', *Journal of Marriage and the Family* 45, 1983, p. 416.

20 Eisler, R.T., *op. cit.*, p. 15.

21 Weitzman, L.J., *op. cit.*, p. xii.

22 Stirling, K.J., 'Women Who Remain Divorced: the Long-Term Economic Consequences', *Social Science Quarterly* 70, 1989, pp. 549-61.

23 Arendell, T., *Mothers and Divorce: Legal, Economic, and Social Dilemmas*, Berkeley: University of California Press, 1986, p. 36.

24 Neely, R., *The Divorce Decision: The Legal and Human Consequences of Ending a Marriage*, New York: McGraw-Hill, 1984, p. 17.

25 Weitzman, L.J., *op. cit.*, p. xii.

26 Abraham, J.H., 'The Divorce Revolution Revisited: A Counter-Revolutionary Critique', *Northern Illinois University Law Review*, 9, 1989, pp. 263, 268, 277, 295.

27 Wallerstein, J.S., 'Women After Divorce: Preliminary Report From a Ten-Year Follow-up', *American Journal of Orthopsychiatry*, 56, 1986, pp. 65-77.

28 Schoenborn, C. and Wilson, B.F., 'Are Married People Healthier? Health Characteristics of Married and Unmarried U.S. Men and Women', paper presented at the American Public Health Association, Boston, Massachusetts, 15 November 1988.

29 See, for instance, Wasserman, I.M., 'The Impact of Divorce on Suicide in the United States 1970-1983', *Family Perspective*, 24, 1990, pp. 61-68.

30 Chesterton, G.K., *The Superstition of Divorce*, 1920, in Marlin, G. (ed.), *et al.*, *Collected Works*, San Francisco, Ignatius Press, 1987, Vol. 4, p. 239.

31 Cohen, L., *op. cit.*, p. 274.

32 Hopps, J.G., 'Is No-Fault Without Fault?', *Social Work*, January-February 1987, p. 4.

33 Study cited by Vance Packard, *Our Endangered Children: Growing Up in a Changing World*, Boston: Little, Brown, 1983, p. 193.

34 See Wallerstein, J.S. and Blakeslee, S., *Second Chances: Men, Women, and Children a Decade After Divorce*, New York: Ticknor & Fields, 1989, p. 13.

35 US Bureau of the Census, *Statistical Abstract of the Unites States: 1990*, 110th ed., Washington: US Government Printing Office, 1993, Table 131.

36 *Ibid.*, Table 69.

37 Arendell, T., *op. cit.*, Table 6, p. 173.

38 See Weitzman, L.J., *op. cit.*, p. 369.

39 Furstenberg, Jr., F.F. and Harris, K.M., 'The Disappearing American Father? Divorce and the Waning Significance of Biological Fatherhood', unpublished paper, University of Pennsylvania, March 1990.

40 Booth, A., 'The State of the American Family', *Journal of Family Issues*, 8 1987, p. 430.

41 McLanahan, S., 'The Long-Term Economic Effects of Family Dissolution', in *When Families Fail .. The Social Costs*, Christensen, B.J. (ed.), Lanham, MD: University Press of America/The Rockford Institute, 1991, pp. 5-25; Angel, R. and Worobey, J.L., 'Single Motherhood and Children's Health', *Journal of Health and Social Behavior*, 29, 1988, pp. 38-52; Zill, N. and Schoenborn, C.A., 'Developmental, Learning and Emotional Problems: Health of Our Nation's Children, United States, 1988', *Advance Data*, No. 190, Vital and Health Statistics of the National Center for Health Statistics, 16 November 1990; Daly, M. and Wilson, M., 'Child Abuse and Other Risks of Not Living With Both Parents', *Ethology and Sociology*, 6, 1985, pp. 197-209; Needle, R.H., Su, S.S. and Doherty, W.J., 'Divorce, Remarriage, and Adolescent Substance Use: A Prospective Longitudinal Study', *Journal of Marriage and the Family*, 52, 1990, pp. 157-59.

42 See McCall, P.L., 'Adolescent and Elderly White Male Suicide Trends: Evidence of Changing Well-Being?', *Journal of Gerontology: Social Sciences*, 46, 1991, pp. 543-51.

43 See 'Family Failure—Summary of a Discussion', in *When Families Fail ... The Social Costs, op. cit.*, p. 98.

44 Neely, R., *op. cit.*, p. 185.

45 *Ibid.*, p. 183.

46 See, for instance, Gallaway, L. and Vedder, R., *Poverty, Income Distribution, The Family and Public Policy*, a study prepared for the Subcommittee on Trade, Productivity, and Economic Growth of the Joint Economic Committee, Congress of the United States, 19 December 1986, Washington: US Government Printing Office, 1986, pp. 84-89; Plotnick, R.D., 'Welfare and Out-of-Wedlock Childbearing: Evidence from the 1980s', *Journal of Marriage and the Family*, 52, 1990, pp. 735-46.

47 Dixon, R.B. and Weitzman, L.J., *op. cit.*, p. 306.

48 Guhring, E., 'Family Law in Transition: Is the Law Changing Too Fast?' *Trial*, April 1981, p. 30.

49 Ward, S.K., 'Tort Claims in Divorce Litigation', *Trial*, November 1988, pp. 68-69.

50 Glenn, N.D., 'The Recent Trend in Marital Success in the United States', *Journal of Marriage and the Family*, 53, 1991, pp. 261-70.

51 Mintz, S., 'Regulating the American Family', *Journal of Family History*, 14, 1989, pp. 387-408.

52 Swan, G.S., 'The Political Economy of American Family Policy, 1945-85', *Population and Development Review*, 12, 1986, p. 752.

53 Chesterton, G.K., *Divorce vs. Democracy*, 1916, in *Collected Works, op. cit.*, Vol. 4, p. 44.

54 Glendon, M.A., *The New Family and the New Property*, Toronto: Butterworths, p. 227.

55 Swan, G.S., *op. cit.*, p. 752.

56 See Johnson, L.A., interview with Craswell, E.,'Discourage Divorce Through Tough State Laws, Senator Says', Tacoma, *News Tribune*, 2 March 1991.

57 Senate Bill No. 1168, 87th General Assembly, State of Illinois, 1991, and 1992.

58 Witcher, P.H., 'Issue: Re-Establishing Fault, as Appropriate, in Divorce', unpublished statement, Chadds Ford, PA 19317, p. 4; see also 'Are Spouses Constitutionally Protected?', *Washington Watch*, April 1991, p. 3.

59 Weitzman, L.J., *op. cit.*, pp. xi, 401.

60 Presser, A.L., *op. cit.*, p. 125.

61 See in this context, testimony of Henry, R.K., on the Revised D.C. Superior Court Child Support Guideline, Judiciary Committee of the District of Columbia City Council, 29 November 1989.

The Family-Values Debate

James Q. Wilson

T HERE are two views about the contemporary American family, one held by the public and the other by policy élites. The public's view is this: the family is the place in which the most basic values are instilled in children. In recent years, however, these values have become less secure, in part because the family has become weaker and in part because rivals for its influence—notably television and movies—have gotten stronger. One way the family has become weaker is that more and more children are being raised in one-parent families, and often that one parent is a teenage girl. Another way is that parents, whether in one- or two-parent families, are spending less time with their children and are providing poorer discipline. Because family values are so important, political candidates should talk about them, though it is not clear that the government can do much about them. Overwhelmingly, Americans think that it is better for children if one parent stays home and does not work, even if that means having less money.[1]

No such consensus is found among scholars or policy-makers. That in itself is revealing. Beliefs about families that most people regard as virtually self-evident are hotly disputed among people whose job it is to study or support families.

A good example of the élite argument began last fall on the front page of the *Washington Post*, where a reporter quoted certain social scientists as saying that the conventional two-parent family was not as important for the healthy development of children as was once supposed. This prompted David Popenoe, a professor at Rutgers who has written extensively on family issues, to publish in the *New York Times* an op-ed piece challenging the scholars cited in the *Post*. Popenoe asserted that 'dozens' of studies had come to the opposite conclusion, and that the weight of the evidence 'decisively' supported the view that two-parent families are better than single-parent families.

Decisively to him, perhaps, but not to others. Judith Stacey, another professor of sociology, responded in a letter to the *Times* that the value of a two-parent family was merely a 'widely shared prejudice' not confirmed by empirical studies; Popenoe, she said, was trying to convert 'misguided nostalgia for "Ozzie-and-Harriet"-land into social-scientific truth.' Arlene and Jerome Skolnick, two more professors, acknowledged that although Popenoe might be correct, saying so publicly would 'needlessly stigmatize children raised in families that don't meet the "Ozzie-and-Harriet" model.' After all, the Skolnicks observed, a man raised outside that model had just been elected President of the United States.

The views of Stacey and the Skolnicks are by no means unrepresentative of academic thinking on this subject. Barbara Dafoe Whitehead recently surveyed the most prominent textbooks on marriage and the family. Here is my paraphrase of her summary of what she found:

> The life course is full of exciting options. These include living in a commune, having a group marriage, being a single parent, or living together. Marriage is one life-style choice, but before choosing it people weigh its costs and benefits against other options. Divorce is a part of the normal family cycle and is neither deviant nor tragic. Rather, it can serve as a foundation for individual renewal and new beginnings. Marriage itself should not be regarded as a special, privileged institution; on the contrary, it must catch up with the diverse pluralistic society in which we live. For example, same-sex marriages often involve more sharing and equality than do heterosexual relationships. But even in the conventional family, the relationships between husband and wife need to be defined after carefully negotiating agreements that protect each person's separate interests and rights.[2]

Many politicians and reporters echo these sentiments and carry the argument one step further. Not only do poor Ozzie and Harriet (surely the most maligned figures in the history of television) stand for nostalgic prejudice and stigmatizing error, they represent a kind of family that in fact scarcely exists. Congresswoman Pat Schroeder has been quoted as saying that only about 7 per cent of all American families fit the Ozzie-and-Harriet model. Our daily newspapers frequently assert that most children will not grow up in a two-parent family. The message is clear: not only is the two-parent family not especially good for children, but fortunately it is also fast disappearing.

Yet whether or not the two-parent family is good for children, it is plainly false that this kind of family has become a historical relic. For while there has been a dramatic increase in the proportion of children, especially black children, who will spend some or even most of their youth in single-parent families, the vast majority of children—nationally, about 73 per cent—live in a home with married parents. Today, the mothers in those families are more likely to work than once was the case, though most do not work full time. (I am old enough to remember that even Harriet worked, at least in real life. She was a singer.)

The proponents of the relic theory fail to use statistics accurately. The way they arrive at the discovery that only 7 per cent of all families fit the Ozzie-and-Harriet model is by calculating what proportion of all families consists *exactly* of a father, mother, and two (not three or four) children and in which the mother never works, not even for two weeks during the year helping out with the Christmas rush at the post office.

The Family and the Role of Women

The language in which the debate over two-parent families is carried on suggests that something more than scholarly uncertainty is at stake. If all we cared about were the effects of one- versus two-parent families on the lives of children, there would still be a debate, but it would not be conducted on op-ed pages in tones of barely controlled anger. Nor would it be couched in slogans about television characters or supported by misleading statistics.

What is at stake, of course, is the role of women. To defend the two-parent family is to defend, the critics worry, an institution in which the woman is subordinated to her husband, confined to domestic chores with no opportunity to pursue a career, and taught to indoctrinate her children with a belief in the rightness of this arrangement. To some critics, the woman here is not simply constrained, she is abused. The traditional family, in this view, is an arena in which men are free to hit, rape, and exploit women. To defend the traditional family is to defend sexism. And since single-parent families are disproportionately headed by black women, criticizing such families is not only sexist but racist.

Perhaps the most influential book on this subject to appear during the 1970s was *The Future of Marriage* by Jessie Bernard, a distinguished scholar. Widely reviewed, its central message was that the first order of business for marriage must be 'mitigating its hazards for women.'

Unlike more radical writers, Bernard thought that the future of marriage was assured, but this would be the case only because marriage would now take many forms. Traditional marriages would persist but other forms would gain (indeed, had already gained) favour—communes, group marriages, the *ménage à trois*, marital 'swinging', unmarried cohabitation, and limited -commitment marriages. (She did not discuss mother-only families as one of these 'options'. Nor did she discuss race.) In principle, no one form was better than another because 'there is nothing in human nature that favors one kind of marriage over another'. In practice, the forms that were best were those that were best for the woman. What might be best for children was not discussed. Children, it would seem, were incidental to marriage, except insofar as their care imposed strains on their parents, especially their mothers.

The main theme of much of the writing about marriage and families during the 1970s and 1980s was that of individual rights. Just as polities were only legitimate when they respected individual rights, so also marriages were worthy of respect only when they were based on a recognition of rights.

This view impressed itself on many who were not scholars, as is evident from an essay published in 1973 in the *Harvard Educational Review*. It urged that the 'legal status of infancy ... be abolished' so that a child would be endowed with all the rights of an adult. Even more, any law that classified people as children and treated them differently from adults 'should be considered suspect'. As a result, the state 'would no longer be able to assume the rationality of regulations based on age'. The author of this essay was Hillary Rodham.

The Evidence Mounts

A rights-based, individualistic view of marriage is questionable in its own terms, but these theoretical questions would become insuperable objections if it could be shown that children are harmed by growing up in mother-only, or communal, or swinging, or divorced households. The academic study of families during the 1970s, however, did not produce an unchallenged body of evidence demonstrating that this was the case. There were several studies that attempted to measure the impact of mother-only families on their children's school attainment, job success, and personal conduct, but many discovered either no effects or ones that were ambiguous or equivocal.

I first became aware of this in the early 1980s when Richard J. Herrnstein and I were writing *Crime and Human Nature*. One of my tasks was to prepare the first draft of the chapter on the effects on crime rates of what were then called broken homes. I fully expected to find a raft of studies showing that growing up in a mother-only home put the child, especially the boy, at risk for criminality.

I did not find what I had expected to find. To be sure, I ran across the familiar fact that men in prison tended disproportionately to come from broken homes, but men in prison also tended to have parents who were themselves criminal and to come from poor, minority backgrounds. Since these factors—class, race, parental criminality, and family status—tended to co-vary, it was not clear that family background had any effect independent of temperament or circumstance. Similarly, Elizabeth Herzog and Cecelia Sudia reviewed eighteen studies of female-headed families carried out between 1950 and 1970. They found that in seven there was more delinquency in father-absent homes, in four there was less, and in seven the results were mixed. Some studies showed boys in father-absent homes failing to develop an appropriate masculine identity and others uncovered no such effect. (There was—and is—ample evidence that children from cold, discordant homes are likely to have plenty of problems, but there are lots of cold, discordant two-parent families.)

Since I wrote that chapter, though, the evidence that single-parent families are bad for children has mounted. There will never be anything like conclusive proof of this proposition unless we randomly assign babies at birth to single- and two-parent families of various economic and ethnic circumstances and then watch them grow up. Happily the laws and customs of this country make such an experiment unlikely. Short of that, the best evidence comes from longitudinal studies that follow children as they grow up in whatever kind of family nature has provided.

One example: when the 5,000 children born in the United Kingdom during the first week of March 1946 were followed for three decades, those raised in families broken by divorce or desertion were more likely than those living in two-parent families to become delinquent.[3]

A second example: for many years, Sheppard Kellam and his colleagues at Johns Hopkins University followed several hundred poor, black, first-grade children in a depressed neighbourhood in Chicago. Each child lived in one of several different family types, depending on how many and what kinds of adults were present. In about one-third of families the mother was the only adult present; in another third there was both a mother and a father. (Only a tiny fraction was headed by a father with no mother present.) The remainder was made up of various combinations of mothers, grandparents, uncles, aunts, adult brothers and sisters, and various unrelated adults. By the time the children entered the third grade, those who lived with their mothers alone were the worst off in terms of their socialization. After ten years, the boys who had grown up in mother-only families (which by then made up about half the total) reported more delinquencies, regardless of family income, than those who had grown up in families with multiple adults, especially a father.[4]

By 1986, when Rolf and Magda Loeber of the University of Pittsburgh reviewed 23 studies assessing the relationship of parental absence (usually, father absence) to juvenile delinquency, they found an effect, though smaller than the one caused by discord within a two-parent family.[5] One problem with their overall conclusion was that they lumped together families where the biological father had never been present with those in which he left, as a result of separation, divorce, or death, while the child was growing up. Inspecting their data suggests that if the latter cases are omitted, the connection between family status and criminality is strengthened a bit: fathers never present create greater hazards than fathers who depart (owing to death or divorce) later in the child's life. The greatest hazard of all is found in families where the parents have the greatest number of problems—they are absent, discordant, rejecting, incompetent, and criminal.

The most recent important study of family structure was done in 1988 by the Department of Health and Human Services. It surveyed the family arrangements of more than 60,000 children living in households all over the country. Interviews were conducted in order to identify any childhood problems in health, schoolwork, and personal conduct. These results were tabulated according to the age, sex, and ethnicity of the child and the income and marital status of the parents.

The results were striking. At every income level save the very highest (over $50,000 per year), for both sexes and for whites, blacks, and Hispanics alike, children living with a never-married or divorced mother were substantially worse off than those living in two-parent families. Compared to children living with both biological parents, children in single-parent families were twice as likely to have been expelled or suspended from school, to display emotional or behavioral problems, and to have problems with their peers; they were also much more likely to engage in antisocial behaviour. These differences were about as wide in households earning over $35,000 a year as they were in those making less than $10,000.[6]

Charles Murray of the American Enterprise Institute has been looking at the people whose lives have been followed by the National Longitudinal Study of Youth (NLSY) since they were in high school (they are now in their late twenties or early thirties). The NLSY not only keeps careful records of the schooling, jobs, and income of these young adults, it also looks at the home environment in which they are raising any children they may have. These home observations rate emotional quality, parental involvement in child care, style of discipline, and the like. The homes, thus observed, can be ranked from best to worst.

Murray has compared the home environments with the economic status of the parents and the legal status of the child. The odds of the children living in the worst home environments were powerfully affected by two things: whether the parents were married when they had the baby and whether they were regular welfare recipients. The child of an unmarried woman who was a chronic welfare recipient had one chance in six of growing up in the worst that is, emotionally the worst environment. The child of a married woman who never went on welfare had only one chance in 42.[7]

Being poor hurts children. Living in a rotten neighbourhood hurts them. Having cold or neglectful parents certainly hurts them. But so also does being illegitimate and living on welfare. This is generally true for whites as well as blacks.

And so also does being a teenage mother. For many years, Frank Furstenberg of the University of Pennsylvania and his colleagues have been following 300 teenage mothers living in Baltimore. What they have found supports the public's view. Teenage girls who have babies fare much worse than ones who postpone child-bearing, and this is true even among girls of the same socio-economic background and academic aptitude. They are more likely to go on welfare, and less likely to enter into a stable marriage. The children of teenage mothers, compared with those of older ones, tend to have more trouble in school, to be more aggressive, and to have less self-control. This is especially true of boys.[8]

We have always had teenage mothers, and in some less-developed societies that is the norm. What is new and troubling about the present situation is the vast increase in the number of teenage mothers and their concentration in the same neighbourhoods. A girl with a baby presents one kind of problem when she is either a rarity or is embedded in an extended family that provides guidance and assistance from older women living with her. She presents a very different and much more serious problem when she is one of thousands of similarly situated youngsters living in the same neighbourhood or public-housing project, trying to maintain an independent household on welfare.

A lot more light was shed on these issues when Sara McLanahan at Princeton and Gary Sandefur at the University of Wisconsin published their careful analysis of the best available longitudinal data bases.[9] There are at least four of these files—the already-mentioned National Longitudinal Study of Youth; the Panel Study of Income Dynamics; the High School and Beyond Study; and the National Survey of Families and Households. McLanahan and Sandefur are looking at the effect of family structure, after controlling for income, race, and education, on such things as a child's chances of graduating from high school, a girl's chances of becoming a teenage mother, and a boy's chances of being idle (that is, neither working nor in school). Their results so far suggest that children who grow up in single-parent families do less well than those who grow up in intact families, and that this is true whether they are white or black, rich or poor, boys or girls. These other factors make a difference—it is better to be white than black, rich than poor—but so does family status.

The Day Care Debate

I think that the American people are right in their view of
families. When they look at the dramatic increase in divorce,
single-parent families, and illegitimate children that has taken
place over the last 30 years, they see families in decline. They
do not need studies to tell them that these outcomes are
generally bad, because they have had these outcomes happen to
them or to people they know. Divorce may sometimes be the
right and necessary remedy for fundamentally flawed marriages
and for the conditions created by an abusive or neglectful
spouse, but in general divorce makes people worse off: the
woman becomes poorer and the children more distressed.
Properly raising a child is an enormous responsibility that often
taxes the efforts and energies of two parents; one parent is
likely to be overwhelmed. Children born out of wedlock are in
the great majority of cases children born into poverty. Millions
of people are living testimony to these bleak facts. If scholars
say that the evidence is not conclusive, so much the worse for
scholars. But now, I believe, scholars are starting to find hard
facts to support popular impressions.

The debate over the effects of family structure continues,
albeit with some prospect of a consensus emerging some time in
the near future. But there is not even a glimmer of such an
accord with respect to the other hot topic in family studies—day
care. The dominant view among child psychologists is that day
care is not harmful. For a long time Professor Jay Belsky of
Pennsylvania State University shared that view. When he
changed his mind, he was excoriated. He is now of the opinion
that day care, especially in the first year of life, is harmful in
some respects to some children.

In a widely-reported 1988 article, Belsky reviewed all the
studies measuring the effect of nonmaternal care on attachment
and social development and concluded that, subject to many
caveats,

> entry into [day] care in the first year of life for twenty hours or
> more per week is a 'risk factor' for the development of insecure
> attachment in infancy and heightened aggressiveness, noncompli-
> ance, and withdrawal in the preschool and early school years.[10]

By 'risk factor' Belsky meant that the child in day care was
somewhat more likely to experience these adverse outcomes than

would a similar child under parental care, especially if the day care was not of high quality.

Some critics argued with Belsky on scientific grounds, saying that the evidence was less clear cut than he suggested, that the measure of emotional well-being he used (observing how a child reacts after it is separated from its mother) was flawed, that children turn out well in cultures where nonparental care is commonplace, and that whatever ill effects exist (if any) do not last.

But many attacked him politically, and even the scholarly critiques had a sharp edge to them. As with family structure, what is at stake in this controversy are not just facts and interpretations but philosophy and policy: if day care has bad effects, then women ought to care for their children in their own homes. And that is a politically incorrect conclusion. Many scholars feel, I believe, that to support the claim of family decline is to give aid and comfort to conservative politicians and religious leaders who bemoan that decline and call for the reassertion of 'traditional values.' In short, what is at stake is Murphy Brown.

The Changing Culture

Both teenage pregnancies and single-parent families have increased dramatically since the 1950s. Changes in the economy and in the provision of welfare benefits explain some of this growth but not all or even most of it. There are no doubt some features peculiar to American society that explain some of it, but since the decline of the family—that is, in lasting marriages and legitimate births—has happened in many nations, it cannot be entirely the result of American policies or peculiarities.

We are witnessing a profound, worldwide, long-term change in the family that is likely to continue for a long time. The causes of that change are not entirely understood, but probably involve two main forces: a shift in the family's economic function and a shift in the culture in which it is embedded. The family no longer is the unit that manages economic production, as it was when agriculture was the dominant form of production, nor is it any longer the principal provider of support for the elderly or education for the young.

At the same time, the family no longer exercises as much

control over its members as it once did, and broader kinship groupings (clans, tribes, and extended families) no longer exercise as much control over nuclear families. Since the Enlightenment, the dominant tendency in legal and philosophical thought has been to emancipate the individual from all forms of tutelage—the state, revealed religion, ancient custom—including the tutelage of kin. This emancipation has proceeded episodically and unevenly, but relentlessly. Liberal political theory has celebrated the individual and constrained the state, but it has been silent about the family.

What is remarkable is how well the family has survived this process. Were the family the mere social convention that some scholars imagine, it would long since have gone the way of cottage industries and the owner-occupied farm, the inevitable victim of the individualizing and rationalizing tendencies of modern life. But, of course, the family is not a human contrivance invented to accomplish some goal and capable of being reinvented or reformulated to achieve different goals.

Family—and kinship generally—are the fundamental organizing facts of all human societies, primitive or advanced, and have been such for tens of thousands of years. The family is the product of evolutionary processes that have selected against people who are inclined to abandon their offspring and for people who are prepared to care for them, and to provide this caring within kinship systems defined primarily along genetic lines. If kinship were a cultural artifact, we could as easily define it on the basis of height, athletic skill, or political status, and children would be raised in all manner of collectives, ranging from state-run orphanages to market-supplied foster homes. Orphanages and foster homes do of course exist, but only as matters of last resort designed (with great public anxiety) to provide care when the biological family does not exist or cannot function.

If the family were merely a convenience and if it responded entirely to economic circumstances, the current debate over family policy would be far less rancorous than it is. Liberals would urge that we professionalize child-rearing through day care; conservatives would urge that we subsidize it through earned-income tax credits. Liberals would define the welfare problem as entirely a matter of poverty and recommend more generous benefits as the solution; conservatives would define it as entirely a matter of dependency and recommend slashing benefits as the solution. Liberals would assume that the problem is that families have too little money, conservatives that families get such money as they have from the state. There would still be a battle, but in the end it would come down to some negotiated compromise involving trade-offs among benefit levels, eligibility rules, and the public-private mix of child-care providers.

But once one conceives of the family problem as involving to a significant degree the conflict between a universal feature of human society and a profound cultural challenge to the power of that institution, the issue takes on a different character. To the extent that one believes in the cultural challenge—that is, in individual emancipation and individual choice—one tends to question the legitimacy and influence of the family. To the extent that one believes in the family, one is led to question some or all parts of the cultural challenge.

That is why the debate over 'family values' has been so strident. On both sides people feel that it is the central battle in the culture war that now grips Americans (or at least American élites). They are absolutely right. To many liberals, family values means a reassertion of male authority, a reduction in the hard-earned rights of women, and a license for abusive or neglectful parents to mistreat their children free of prompt and decisive social intervention. For some liberals, family values means something even more troubling: that human nature is less malleable than is implied by the doctrine of environmental determinism and cultural relativism—that it is to some significant degree fixed, immutable. To many conservatives, family values is the main line of resistance against homosexual marriages, bureaucratized child care, and compulsory sex education in the schools. For some conservatives, the family means a defense against the very idea of a planned society.

The War over Commitment

Now, reasonable people—say, the typical mother or father—will take a less stark view of the alternatives. They will agree with conservatives that the family is the central institution of society, incapable of being replaced or even much modified without disastrous consequences. They will be troubled by same-sex marriages, upset by teenage girls becoming mothers, angered by public subsidies for illegitimate births, and outraged by the distribution of condoms and explicit sex-education manuals to elementary-school children. But they will agree with many liberals that we ought not to confine women to domestic roles or make them subservient to male power and that we ought to recognize and cope with the financial hardships that young couples have today when they try to live on one income in a big city.

On one issue most parents will squarely identify with the conservative side, and it is, in my view, the central issue. They will want our leaders, the media, television programmes, and motion pictures to take their side in the war over what the family is. It is not one of several alternative life-styles; it is not an arena in which rights are negotiated; it is not an old-fashioned and reactionary barrier to a promiscuous sex life; it is not a set of cost-benefit calculations. *It is a commitment.*

It is a commitment required for child-rearing and thus for any realistic prospect of human happiness. It is a commitment that may be entered into after romantic experimentation and with some misgivings about lost freedoms, but once entered into it is a commitment that persists for richer or for poorer, in sickness and in health, for better or for worse. It is a commitment for which there is no feasible substitute, and hence no child ought lightly to be brought into a world where that commitment from both parents is absent. It is a commitment that often is joyfully enlivened by mutual love and deepening friendship, but it is a commitment even when these things are absent.

There is no way to prepare for the commitment other than to make it. The idea that a man and a woman can live together without a commitment in order to see if they would like each other after they make the commitment is preposterous. Living together may inform you as to whether your partner snores or is an alcoholic or sleeps late; it may be fun and exciting; it may even be the best you can manage in an imperfect world. But it is not a way of finding out how married life will be, because married life is shaped by the fact that the couple has made a solemn vow before their family and friends that this is for keeps and that any children will be their joint and permanent responsibility. It changes everything.

Despite high divorce rates and a good deal of sleeping around, most people understand this. Certainly women understand it, since one of their most common complaints about the men they know is that they will not make a commitment. You bet they won't, not if they can get sex, cooking, and companionship on a trial basis, all the while keeping their eyes peeled for a better opportunity elsewhere. Marriage is in large measure a device for reining in the predatory sexuality of males. It works quite imperfectly, as is evident from the fact that men are more likely than women to have extramarital affairs and to abandon their spouses because a younger or more exciting possibility has presented herself. But it works better than anything else mankind has been able to invent.

Because most people understand this, the pressures, economic and cultural, on the modern family have not destroyed it. And this is remarkable, considering the spread of no-fault divorce laws. The legal system has, in effect, said, 'Marriage is not a commitment; it is a convenience. If you feel yours is inconvenient, we will make it easy for you to get out of it.' This radical transformation of family law occurred, as Mary Ann Glendon of the Harvard Law School has shown, in many industrialized countries at about the same time. It may or may not have caused the rise in the divorce rate, but it certainly did nothing to slow it down.

The legal system has also altered child-custody rules so that, instead of being automatically assigned to the father (as was the case in the 19th century, when the father was thought to 'own' all the family's property including the child), the child is now assigned by the judge on the basis of its 'best interests'. In the vast majority of cases, that means with the mother. I sometimes wonder what would happen to family stability if every father knew for certain that, should the marriage end, he would have to take custody of the children. My guess is: more committed fathers.

These cultural and legal changes, all aimed at individualizing and empowering family members, have had an effect. In 1951, 51 per cent of all Americans agreed with the statement that 'parents who don't get along should not stay together because there are children in the family'. By 1985, 86 per cent agreed.[11] Still, these changes have not devastated modern families. The shopping malls, baseball stadiums, and movie theatres are filled with them doing what families have always done. That fact is a measure of the innate power of the family bond.

Yet the capacity for resisting these changes is unequally distributed in society. Christopher Jencks of Northwestern University puts it this way:

Now that the mass media, the schools, and even the churches have begun to treat single parenthood as a regrettable but inescapable part of modern life, we can hardly expect the respectable poor to carry on the struggle against illegitimacy and desertion with their old fervor. They still deplore such behavior, but they cannot make it morally taboo. Once the two-parent norm loses its moral sanctity, the selfish considerations that always pulled poor parents apart often become overwhelming.[12]

Culture and Politics

The central issue in family policy is whether or not it will be animated entirely by an economic view of family functions and consist entirely of economic solutions to family needs. The principal source of domestic social-policy advice to Bill Clinton during his presidential campaign was the Progressive Policy Institute (PPI), and in particular Elaine Kamarck and William Galston. 'The best antipoverty program for children is a stable, intact family', they wrote in their report, *Mandate for Change*. Though not neglecting economic measures, such as a tax credit for each child and an earned-income tax credit to supplement the wages of the working poor, the PPI urged that the divorce laws be changed to protect children better, that efforts be intensified to promote parental responsibility for child care, that pregnant women who use drugs be required to undergo periodic drug testing, and that the earnings of absent parents be taxed to pay for their children. And the report called for the President to use his bully pulpit to reinforce the importance of intact and caring families.

Only Galston of all those connected with the PPI was appointed to even a moderately significant position in the Clinton administration (he joined the White House domestic-policy staff). Clinton's Secretary of Health and Human Services, Donna Shalala, had virtually nothing to say about these matters in her confirmation hearing before the Senate Finance Committee.

The truth of the matter is that the most important features of family life are beyond the reach of policy. The recently passed family-leave bill in large measure merely ratifies opportunities that large firms have been granting to their employees for some time; it will make things a bit easier for middle-class mothers but will do little for poor, teenage ones. The far more contentious issue of welfare reform will not be so easily resolved, but it is hard to imagine any feasible change in the existing rules that will make much of a difference in the chances of a child being born out of wedlock. Expanding the earned-income tax credit may help poor working parents, but do we really want single mothers of two-year-old children to work? Tightening the divorce laws may be a good idea, but it will not make much difference to parents who never got married in the first place. Improving the system for collecting child-support payments is a good idea, but many fathers who desert their children have little money to be collected and, in any event, this is not likely to convert uncommitted impregnators into committed fathers.

I suspect that the culture of the family will have to be rebuilt from the bottom up. Certainly Robert Woodson, head of the National Center for Neighborhood Enterprise, thinks so. He and his associates have been energetically pursuing this goal by supporting local church-related groups that try to encourage men to take responsibility for their children. There are many other local efforts to get men to marry their pregnant lovers and to sign the birth certificates of their children.

But these efforts proceed against the cultural grain, or at least against the grain of the high culture. When the people who deliver mocking attacks on 'traditional family values' are the same ones who endorse condom distribution among elementary-school children, the average parent is led to wonder whether he or she is being a sucker for trying to stay together and raise the kids. Most Americans, I would guess, understand very clearly the difference between a traditional family and an oppressive one; they want the former but not the latter. Most women, I would guess, can distinguish very easily between the rights they have won and the obligations they retain; they cherish both and see no fundamental conflict between them, except the inescapable problem that there is not enough time for everything and so everyone must make choices.

It is extraordinary how well most husbands and wives have held up in the face of constant taunts comparing them to Ozzie and Harriet. The family life that most Americans want is regarded by the eminences of the media and the academy as a cartoon life, fit only for ridicule and rejection. When the history of our times is written, this raging cultural war will deserve careful attention, for it is far more consequential than any of the other cleavages that divide us.

Many Americans hope that our leaders will stand up for 'traditional family values', by which they mean, not male supremacy, spouse abuse, or docile wives, but the overriding importance of two-parent families that make child care their central responsibility. Nobody should conceive a child that he and she are not emotionally ready to care for. The best, albeit an imperfect, sign of that readiness is the marriage vow. Let us say that it is wrong—not just imprudent, but wrong—to bear children out of wedlock. Such statements may elicit dismayed groans from sitcom producers and ideological accusations from sociology professors, but at least the people would know that our leaders are on their side.

Notes

1   Evidence for these beliefs can be found in the poll data gathered in the *American Enterprise*, September/October 1992, pp. 85-86.

2   Paraphrased from Whitehead, B.D., *The Expert's Story of Marriage*, Institute for American Values, Publication No. WP14, August 1992, pp. 11-12. Whitehead supplies references to the texts she summarizes. She does not endorse—just the opposite!—the views she has compiled.

3   Wadsworth, M.E.J., *Roots of Delinquency*, Barnes & Noble, 1979.

4   Kellam, S. *et al.*, 'The Long-Term Evolution of the Family Structure of Teenage and Older Mothers', *Journal of Marriage and the Family*, Vol. 44, 1982, pp. 539-54; Kellam, S. *et al.*, 'Family Structure and the Mental Health of Children', *Archives of General Psychiatry*, Vol. 34, 1977, pp. 1012-22; Ensminger, M. *et al.*, 'School and Family Origins of Delinquency: Comparisons By Sex' in Van Dusen, K.T. and Mednick, S.A. (eds.), *Prospective Studies of Crime and Delinquency*, Kluwer-Nijhoff, 1983.

5   Loeber, M. and Loeber, R., 'Family Factors as Correlates and Predictors of Juvenile Conduct Problems and Delinquency' in Tonry, M. and Morris, N. (eds.), *Crime and Justice: An Annual Review of Research*, University of Chicago Press, 1986, pp. 29-149.

6 Dawson, D.A.,'Family Structure and Children's Health: United States, 1988', *Vital and Health Statistics*, Series 10, No. 178, June 1991.

7 Murrey, C., 'Reducing Poverty and Reducing the Underclass: Different Problems, Different Solutions', paper presented to the Conference on Reducing Poverty in America, 15 January 1993, at the Anderson Graduate School of Management, UCLA.

8 Furstenberg Jr., F.F., Brookes-Gunn, J. and Chase-Lansdale, L., 'Teenage Pregnancy and Child-Bearing', *American Psychologist*, Vol. 44, 1989, pp. 313-20.

9 McLanahan, S. and Sandefur, G., *Growing up With a Single Parent*, Harvard University Press, 1994.

10 Belsky, J., 'The "Effects" of Infant Day Care Reconsidered', *Early Childhood Research Quarterly*, Vol. 3, 1988, pp. 235-72. For a response see Field, T., *Infancy*, Harvard University Press, 1990, pp. 90-93.

11 Popenoe, D., 'The Family Condition of America', paper prepared for a Brookings Institution seminar on values and public policy, March 1992, citing a study by Norvel Glenn.

12 Jencks, C., 'Deadly Neighborhoods', the *New Republic*, 13 June 1988, pp. 23-32.

Available for Half-Price

The Family: Is It Just Another Lifestyle Choice?, Jon Davies (Editor), Brigitte Berger and Allan Carlson £6.95, 120pp, 1993, ISBN: 0-255 36276-5

Three essays examine the consequences for individuals and for society of the breakdown of the traditional family. They argue that the family is not just another 'lifestyle choice', but vital to Western civilisation.

"The report says that society is paying a heavy price for the belief that the family is just another lifestyle choice." *The Times*

Equal Opportunities: A Feminist Fallacy, Caroline Quest (Editor), *et al.* £6.95, 111pp, June 1992, ISBN: 0-255 36272 2

"Laws banning sex discrimination and promoting equal pay at work damage the interests of women the Institute of Economic Affairs claims today."
The Daily Telegraph

"Let us not above all be politically correct. Let us not become overheated because the Institute of Economic Affairs has brought out a startling report entitled *Equal Opportunities: A Feminist Fallacy*." *The Times*

God and the Marketplace, Jon Davies (Editor), £4.90, 145pp, 1993
Essays by Rev. John Kennedy, Secretary, Division of Social Responsibility, Methodist Church; Bishop John Jukes, Roman Catholic Bishop of Strathearn; Professor Michael Novak, Professor Richard Roberts, Rev. Simon Robinson

---

"certainly worth reading for Novak alone." *The Tablet*

"Christian theologians welcome the economic role of the market and endorse wealth creation as a primary good." *The Daily Telegraph*

The Emerging British Underclass, Charles Murray with Frank Field MP, Joan Brown, Alan Walker and Nicholas Deakin £5.95, 82pp, May 1990

"Mr Murray... calls himself a visitor from a plague area, come to see if the disease is spreading." *The Daily Telegraph*

"Britain has a small but growing underclass of poor people cut off from the values of the rest of society and prone to violent, anti-social behaviour." *The Times*

Available for Half-Price

Liberating Women ... From Modern Feminism, Caroline Quest (Ed), Norman Barry, Mary Kenny, Patricia Morgan, Joan Kennedy Taylor, Glenn Wilson £6.95, 101pp, 1994, ISBN 0-255 36353-2

Caroline Quest argues that 'power feminism' ends up having as little relevance to most women as the 'victim feminism' it is directed against. It is, she says, 'for pre-maternal young women' and 'is of little relevance and help to the realities of life for the majority of real women'.

"It would be a mistake ... to take anything but seriously the essay "Double income, no kids: the case for a family wage" by the sociologist Patricia Morgan."

Margot Norman, *The Times*

The Moral Foundations of Market Institutions, John Gray, with Chandran Kukathas, Patrick Minford and Raymond Plant, £7.95, 142pp, Feb 1992, ISBN: 0-255 36271-4

Distinguished Oxford philosopher, John Gray, examines the moral legitimacy of the market economy. While upholding the value of the market economy he insists on the importance of an 'enabling' welfare state.

"one of the most intelligent and sophisticated contributions to modern conservative philosophy."
The Times

"This powerful tract ... maps out a plausible middle ground for political debate."
Financial Times

The De-moralization of Society: From Victorian Virtues to Modern Values, Gertrude Himmelfarb, £12.50, 314pp, March 1995, ISBN: 0-255 36359-1

"Gertrude Himmelfarb is one of the world's most knowledgeable scholars of the British Victorian period." *The Sunday Telegraph*

"Gertrude Himmelfarb is one of America's most distinguished intellectual historians. This book will only enhance that reputation." William J. Bennett

Farewell to the Family? Public Policy and Family Breakdown in Britain and the USA, PATRICIA MORGAN, £9.00 175pp, Jan 1995, ISBN: 0-255 36356-7

"Tougher policies to promote family life are being demanded by Tory MPs following a report accusing the Government of discriminating against married couples in favour of lone parents."

The Daily Telegraph

ORDER FORM—EVERYTHING HALF-PRICE

Title	Normal Price	Offer Price	Qty	£
Families Without Fatherhood (2nd Edition)	£7.95	£3.95		
Rising Crime and the Dismembered Family	£5.95	£2.95		
Reinventing Civil Society	£7.95	£3.95		
A Moral Basis for Liberty	£4.95	£2.45		
The Family: Just Another Lifestyle Choice?	£6.95	£3.45		
Equal Opportunities: A Feminist Fallacy	£6.95	£3.45		
Moral Foundations of Market Institutions	£7.95	£3.95		
The Emerging British Underclass	£5.95	£2.95		
Farewell to the Family	£9.00	£4.50		
Underclass: the Crisis Deepens	£5.99	£2.95		
God and the Marketplace	£4.90	£2.45		
The De-moralisation of Society	£12.50	£6.25		
Liberating Women From Modern Feminism	£6.95	£3.45		

Please add 50p P&P per book up to a
maximum of £4.00

Subtotal:
P&P:
Total:

I enclose a cheque for £...................... payable to the Institute of Economic Affairs ☐

Please debit my Mastercard/Visa/Amex/Diner's card for £...................... ☐

Number: ....

Expiry Date: ....

Name: ....

Address: ....

....

....

*Please return to **IEA Health and Welfare Unit, Institute of Economic Affairs,**
2 Lord North Street, Westminster, London SW1P 3LB*